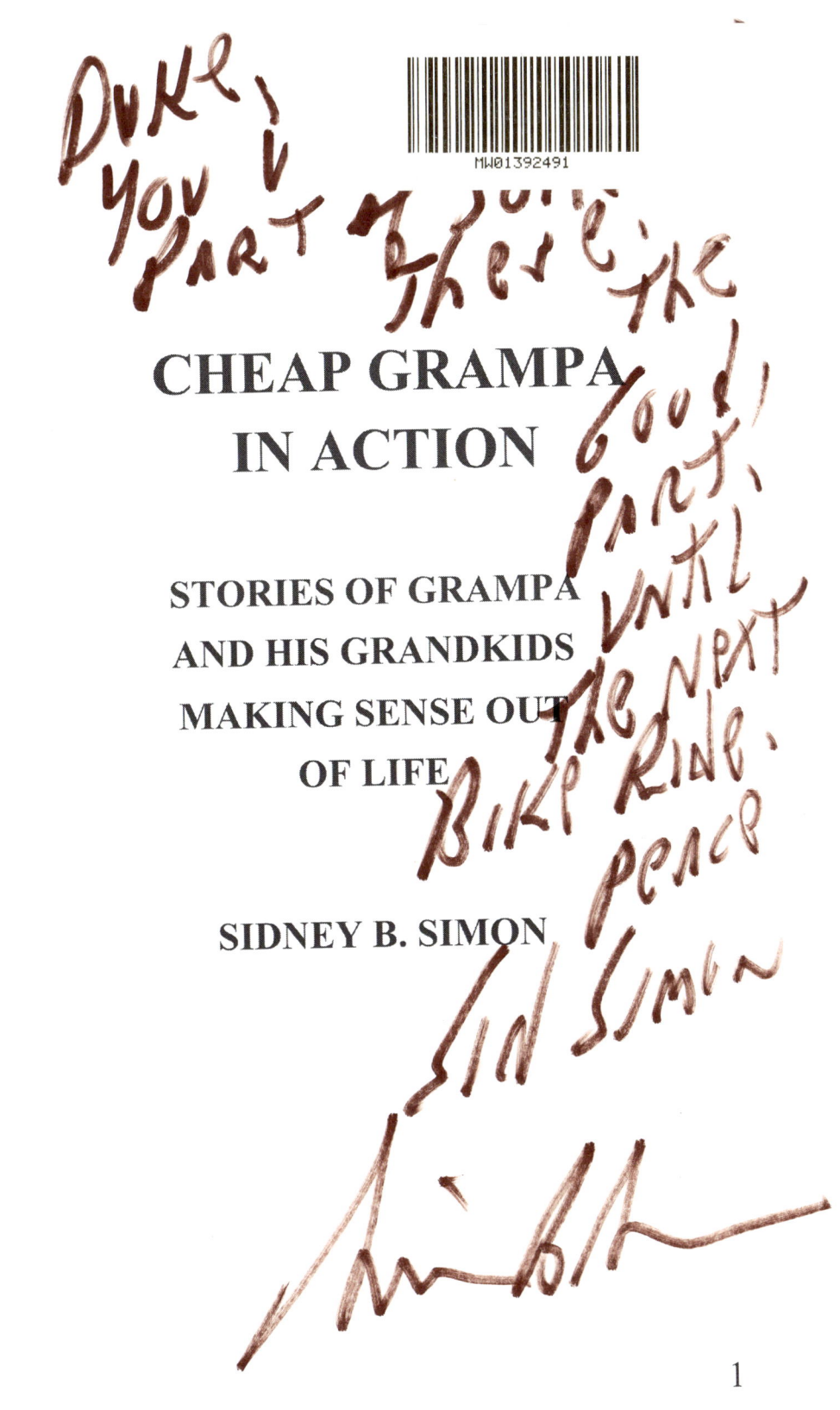

CHEAP GRAMPA IN ACTION

STORIES OF GRAMPA AND HIS GRANDKIDS MAKING SENSE OUT OF LIFE

SIDNEY B. SIMON

Cover photo by Emil Neuman

Cover design by Marianne Preger-Simon

Copyright © 2012 SIDNEY B. SIMON
All rights reserved.
ISBN-13: 978-1469998565
ISBN-10: 1469998564

TABLE OF CONTENTS

	page	
Dedication		6
Who I Am - Album One		8
I'm the Cheap Grampa		9
The Interview		12
Social Scene – Album Two		24
Magic		25
Grampa Fulfills the Condition		32
Grampa Gets Help on a Personal		36
It Hinges		42
Doubt		48
Yogurt Aisle		51
What Should I Do		55
Finding Treasures – Album Three		59
At the Flea Market		60
At the Dump		64
Corn		69
The Bird Feeder		72
Bike Adventures – Album Four		77
Library		78
Grampa, Phoebe, & the Smoker		81
Time for Helmet Day		87
Another Helmet Mission		93
Howl		98
Good Deeds – Album Five		105
At the Salvation Army		106
Camp		109

Band	112
Off to Do a Mitzvah	117
Cheap Grampa & the Call Center Miracle	122
Religion at Starbucks	125

<u>Life Lessons</u> – Album Six	128

County Fair	129
Vocabulary Drill	131
Shade	136
Validations Defined & in Action	141
The Traffic Cop	146

<u>Family Phone Calls</u>–Album Seven	150

Not Really	151
Doctors	156
Transitions	161
Being Taken In	165
Fire	168

<u>Reminiscences</u> – Album Eight	172

Looking Back-Pocusset Street	173
Ideas About Birthday Presents	181
Cheap Grampa & the Cruise Ship	183
Thanks	189
Cheap Grampa, Lark, & Moms	193
Cheap Grampa & the Thing Called Christmas	187
Dog	201

<u>Extravagant Claims</u>–Album Nine	205

Laundry	206
Hallowe'en	209
Grampa & Phoebe Go to a Restaurant	214
Cheap Grampa at the Post Office	220

Reflections – Album Ten 224

Peaches 225
Leaving Florida 227

And Also… 230

Guess What 231

In the End 233

Catastrophe 234

Acknowledgements 237

About the Author 239

Dedication

This book is dedicated to grandfathers, everywhere. Do you remember yours? Were you lucky enough to have two of them? Were they active in your life?

Clearly, each and every one of us was shaped by who our grandfathers were. Mine were immigrants, with all of that coming over in steerage, making sense out of a whole new world, with a language they couldn't speak, without a familiar culture, and yet having to carve out a living here, so often without the necessary skills, skills that were so different from the ones they left behind. It shaped me.

I was a kid during the Great Depression. My dad was a blue-collar worker who was yanked out of school at the end of the third grade to "Go to work, and bring in some money for the family." My mother was lucky enough to get through the fourth grade, and worked from then on until she was sixteen, when she and my dad married.

From then on, my mother ran a boarding house to supplement the hourly wage my father brought home. Six extra beds made up the boarding house. There were twelve people at the dinner table every night. And the person who would grow up to be Cheap Grampa did all of her basic shopping. She trained me well, and she trained me hard. I read the weekly grocery store ads, circled the bargains, and brought them home. She never left the house during the week. I did it for her.

So, here's to all of us who got through the depression, lived through the wars, gave thanks to the G.I. bill, and managed to raise a family; who, as the years unfolded, gave us the amazing grand kids, some of whom have threads in the fictional grand kids in these stories. One of them is only three months old, and he's already in the story about the Post Office.

This Cheap Grampa has become financially secure enough so that I can easily be generous now, even while maintaining buying habits from childhood. And I love thinking I can still act out being cheap and fool those grand kids into believing it.

So to all of you who found yourselves in these stories, I dedicate this book to *you*.

Sidney B. Simon, Sanibel, Florida and Hadley, Massachusetts, 2011

ALBUM ONE

WHO I AM

I'm The Cheap Grampa

Yes, I'm the Cheap Grampa. You know why? If one of my kids buys me a shirt, I put it on. See how it feels and then I give it a try. I wear it when I go out, a couple of times, to the library, to see what reaction I get in public. But I always leave the price tag on. I like seeing them twisting in the wind.

One of the grand kids, the second oldest one, is quick to say, "Grampa, you're supposed to cut the tags off on a new shirt."

And she gets my canned response. "I know. I know, honey, but if it doesn't feel right, and if the price tags are still dangling, I can always take it back, and get no arguments from the poor clerk who has to deal with 'Returns.'"

"But Grampa, it will smell like it's been worn."

"So, what if it's been worn? And, me, I don't smell, and I make sure there are no ketchup stains on it."

"Oh, Grampa!" She gives up. I think I taught her something, so then we take off for a bike ride together. I always bring two plastic bags. One for any cans we find that we can get a refund on. She gets to keep the money. And the other bag for all the debris and litter we find. I'm cheap, but a good citizen, too.

We end the bike ride at the supermarket, where we turn in our cans, and recycle what can be recycled, and then throw what's left in the supermarket's trash bin. We find a bench outside, drink from our non-plastic water bottles we filled up at home, and she and I sit down and start circling what's on sale in the big supermarket flyer.

She says, excitedly, "Grampa, look, 'Buy one get two free!'" That kid knows how to warm my heart. Even if it's something we never eat so we never buy, but today we do. It's on sale, and I'm trying to set a good example.

I validate her. "Good going, darling. Nice job. I know your mother will help us figure out how to use up those three packages of 'Imitation Crab Meat'. Let's go compare what it would have cost if we bought real crab meat." We do, and the results are 'awesome' as she says. She adds, "Good going, Grampa. Nice job. I can't wait to tell the whole family how we saved $17.95."

She adds, "But, Gramps, my mother wouldn't let me eat that junk. I read the labels. If you read what's in it, you wouldn't eat it, either, Gramps, even if it was cheap. And don't think we can give it to the cats. We don't even let *them* eat things with red dye in them."

That's when I give her the 'Depression Talk'. "You don't know what it was like as a kid growing up in the Depression."

She plays with me. "Did you grow up depressed, Grampa? Did you take Ritalin or something?"

"You kidding? I'm not talking depression. I'm talking the Great Depression. I mean we were poor. We were so poor."

She knows her lines, and feeds them to me, perfectly. "How poor were you, Grampa?"

"So poor my mother sent me out to collect 'road kill' on the highway so she could make us meatloaf."

"Oh, Grampa, I'm so sad. Having to eat meatloaf instead of steak."

I tell her, "And that's not all. One of my jobs was to pick the moths out of the 'reduced for quick sale' flour before she baked bread."

My granddaughter gets in the last words. "Your bicycle didn't have tires, and you rode it until the rims wore down to nothing but spokes left to ride on."

"What?" I ask. "Were you there? Well, kid, let's bike home before the rats attack our buy one, get two free genuine fake crab meats." We pedal like mad keeping our eyes out for more discarded cans and abandoned McDonald's styrofoam. What day could have been more perfect for any Cheap Grampa?

Cheap Grampa and the College Graduate Granddaughter

They hadn't seen each other since family reunion, but with a lot of juggling, they both ended up back in her home town, Ithaca, N.Y. Cheap Grampa was excited. Way back when she was little, they had been really close buddies. Little rituals they had, filled almost every visit. There were ceremonial bike rides together. Lunch at her school, walks through the gorges. Swimming in season. And always a visit together to the library and the children's bookstore. Happened every time.

And there was the Counting Game. Collecting points. Red cars spotted on their walks to the Village Center. She must have been six years old when it started, and a quick spotter she was. She got points for designated vehicles. One for red cars, and two points for red pickups. Funny discussions about maroon cars or trucks. And why couldn't she get three points for big dump trucks and maybe four for trailer trucks, as long as they were red.

But, no matter how many points, and what else there was to see, the first store they went to was always the Dollar Store. She knew the rules. She had to walk up and down all the aisles, look at everything, and pick out three things. Then, the torturesome ritual of rank ordering her picks, because she still got only one dollar to spend, but on anything she wanted. After the choice, she put back the other two things. Occasionally, if the visit was long enough, and Cheap Grampa was free to sneak back to the Dollar Store, he just might pick up her two rejects, buy them, and slip them under her pillow before he left.

She was waiting for him on the porch when he pulled up. Another ritual was to call into the house when he was at Whitney Point, about twenty miles down the highway, giving them a warning. He'd be there in a half hour. The timing was perfect. She galloped down the porch steps and pulled him out of his car.

"Oh, Grampa, I'm so glad to see you. I've missed you. How was the trip? Did you see any red dump trucks? They're worth three points."

"Seeing you should be worth twenty points even if you got an orange sweat shirt on. What team plays in orange football jerseys?" he asked. She quickly answered, "Oh, I know, the team from Orange, Massachusetts." And on that she gave him the biggest hug, and said, "But I got this one from an old boyfriend from Princeton. Welcome, welcome. Come in. I made you a banana smoothie."

"Sure, sure, I drive five hours, hoping I would get a kumquat fudge smoothie, and all I get is banana, banana, banana."

She laughed, and said, "Actually, we didn't have any bananas, but I found a peach and it's in there, instead. Promise me you won't taste the difference."

"I promise. Like always. You ask and I promise."

At that point she took the first picture of the afternoon. "There," she said. "I nailed you. I'll caption this one, 'Promise, Promise.' And, Gramps, no, despite your cheapness, I will never forget this glorious camera you gave me. Look. It's hardly dented. And it's been to Mexico in my senior year at high school, and with me through four years of college."

"And, it still takes pictures? Amazing. Mexico and four years of college, and about forty boyfriends?"

"Nah, just thirty-nine, Gramps, and all because none of them was thrifty, frugal and cheap like you. Which reminds me, about my application for Graduate School. We'll have to talk, because I have to submit an interesting interview with some

13

member of my family, an in-depth interview, on one topic, only."

Cheap Grampa smiled. "Your mother would be perfect. An in-depth interview on how to raise children as great as you and your sisters. And if she won't do it, your father would make a super interviewee."

"Nopes, Gramps, I'm gonna do it on you. On you, because that will guarantee that I get into the program. It will be so fascinating that it will probably be the only paper that the admissions person will want to read that day. I will have made his or her day."

"I'm game," he said, taking out two shopping bags of stuff he brought, along with his old suitcase she remembered from so many times. "But are you going to let me try to get up those stairs with two shopping bags and one suitcase?"

She reached for all three. "Of course not. I'm big strong squaw woman. And you get my room tonight, and I get to sleep with my sister, who snores, but it will be fun. We'll talk all night. And after your smoothie, you and I will talk all afternoon, until school's out and everybody gets home."

He stood looking around the yard. "First, I have to know, what depth topic are you going to interview me about? How about my respectable academic career up to the sixth grade? Maybe my 25,000 miles on a BMW motorcycle in Europe? My life in the Navy during WW II? What? What tickles your depths, woman?"

"All those are interesting, of course, Gramps. You're interesting. It's not even a question." She put the shopping bags and suitcase down on the porch and went to him for another hug. "But I want to do an interview that maybe I'll publish in the New Yorker, or sell to Esquire, somewhere where the world will see it."

"Maybe I won't want the world to see it."

"Nonsense, you old ham. My questions will give you lots of chances to moralize, or to be kinder, to teach the people who read it, how to grow up to be a ripe old eighty-four year old with a zest for life that will make any of them envious and deeply curious."

Cheap Grampa stood there and grinned at her. "After all I've done for you, dollar store after dollar store, filled your bike tires with air, once took you to a Chinese all you can eat buffet restaurant, and gave you that slightly used camera, you still haven't told me what the depth interview you're going to do is about. Where's the topic, granddaughter?"

"Well, I did a lot of thinking about this, sitting on the porch waiting for you. I bet you didn't drive right through Whitney Point. I bet you stopped at the Family Dollar Store. I know you. So I had an extra half hour to design the interview."

He laughed. "Well there was a big 'Clearance' sign out front."

"Say no more. I know what that word does to you. I'm sympathetic. And funny enough, that's the topic."

"What? Sympathetic? If it's about me, I don't think the topic fits."

"Oh, you're still such a sweet silly goose. The topic is Cheap. Cheap, cheap."

"You sound like a bird your cousin is re-habbing. Have I got stories to tell you about the Bird Woman of Vermont. But later. So the topic is cheap, cheap, cheap? I like it."

She gave him another hug. She always did that kind of thing. "I don't mean three cheeps. I just think there is an audience out

15

there, especially among the kids who came to the family reunion, who would like to really know, 'How My Grandfather Became the Cheap Grandfather he is.'"

"And you'll be sympathetic?"

"Totally. I love you. And you know it. I always have, even if you're fraudulent, you and your cheap schtick. The depth interview will get to the bottom of it. I have my pad, and my magic marker. I'll write big. You can see what I write, so slide into the swing on the porch here, I'll bring your smoothie out, and then I'll sit on the steps and fire the first question at you. Are you ready?"

"I've been driving five hours. Do you mind if I go up and have a cheap pee? I won't waste any water. And I'll be right back."

"Sure. And, Gramps, we've had a lot of rain this summer. The well is full. Whoopee. You can even flush this time."

"Wow, you really are sympathetic. Ho, ho. I promise, I'll be right back. You just wait. What answers you'll hear tumbling from my cheap lips!"

"And while you're in the john, I'll bring your things up to my room."

"Thanks, kid, that's so like you. You've always been easy to love. So before the interview, do you want to do a quick trip to the Dollar Store? "

"No way, I'm going to get you a smoothie, and then we're interviewing, baby."

"Well, then, how about going to see one of those gorgeous gorges that I'm so fond of in your fair city?"

"No, Gramps, maybe we'll go for a swim when we finish the interview." She walked to the kitchen. He said, "Ok, I give in." And he slipped up stairs.

When he came back down, he found a pillow to sit on already waiting for him on the top step. She handed him his smoothie. "Thanks, honey. This is really nice here. And you're here. I'm here. And I can look at you when you ask your questions, and you can look right at me and study my face when I answer. This is good. Thanks, honey. For a lot of things. One of them is for making me feel so important that you wanted to do this interview. And thanks for the welcome, and the non-banana smoothie, and oh, all the good memories, as well."

She found her pillow, picked up her notebook, and got ready to go to work.

"This is a mighty good smoothie, Robin."

"And organic. Mom is very particular."

He said, "And I know it only costs twice as much as non-organic."

She said, "A perfect segue to the first question."

He said, "And you're sure you don't want to go to the Dollar Store?"

"Grampa. I'm not wanting to send you to the timeout room."

"Oh, yeah, I forgot you are a professional Nanny, and damn good at it, I hear."

"Yeah, you heard it from me. I told you how damn good at it I am, and now I want to get into graduate school, and this interview is one of my admission requirements. First question."

"I'm ready, I'm ready."

"It's simple really. Grampa, how did you become the Cheap Grampa?"

He grew silent for a moment. She watched his face. His eyes got a little misty, but he said. "Good question. You've heard some of this before. If I repeat, you'll stop me."

"No, I won't stop you. I want to hear any of it, all of it, again, and maybe again after that." Now *her* eyes got a little misty.

They reached out and touched hands.

He said, "You're good, Robin. So I begin, in the beginning. I was born in 1927. And shortly thereafter, the Great Depression engulfed us. I was their third kid, ten years younger than my sister, and five years younger than my brother. Our dad was a blue-collar worker. Drove a truck for a wholesale dry cleaning company. Our mother ran the famous boarding house. Twelve people to feed every night. Twelve beds to make each day. Twelve sets of sheets to wash and iron every Monday. And always the anxiety that there would not be enough money to cover the Building and Loan. They never explained to me what a Building and Loan was, but I knew it was that thing that generated lots of anxiety. I thought it had huge teeth and a forked tongue and a crocodile's body.

"My dad had been yanked out of school in the third grade. My mother's parents, more gracious, let her finish the fourth grade. My dad and mother got married when she was sixteen. Money was the center of almost every discussion in that house, and certainly the center of most of the anger and arguments."

Robin looked hard at him, and said, "That explains a lot of it, Gramps. But I know there's more. You could have grown up really damaged by all of that, and ended up at your age, grumpy, frumpy and angry at the world. But none of us sees you as any of those. And we accept that you prefer the Dollar

Store to Neiman-Marcus. So how do you explain your ebullience, sunny disposition, and deep down generosity?"

"What, what, you buttering me up to get a better camera than the one I gave you when you were in high school?"

She said, smiling, "If you don't recognize a genuine validation, I'm giving you a homework assignment to go re-read one of your books."

"Ok, ok, but I have been thinking, maybe a new camera might be something you can use."

"We'll talk. Later. Back to the interview. What contributed to the difference, Gramps?"

"I've thought about it. Who hasn't tried to figure out what made the differences in their lives. Well, one of them was that it fell to me, at the boarding house, to do almost all of my mother's shopping. I must have been seven or eight when I started. And I got very good at it. She didn't even have to give me a list, after a while. I would check to see myself how low she was on Crisco, coffee, sugar, flour, canned peaches, pears, plums. And I would go and get them. But not until I read the grocery ads in the papers, to know where to get the cheapest. Grocery shopping was one afternoon, after school, every week. And other days, I did the butcher run, and the bakery run, which meant buying day old bread, half-price. Milk was delivered, and a 'huckster' came around one day a week with vegetables and fruit. It all worked out."

"But how did that shopping stuff help shape you?" she asked, but he could see on her face, she already knew the answer. He said, "Because it made me feel important, like I mattered. Think about it. How does self-esteem get established? All of us need to believe that we matter, that we make a difference and, of course, that we belong. My shopping did that for me. Even on an afternoon when I forgot something she needed. All I had to do was run back down the hill and get it. Even slipping up made me feel powerful. A problem comes up, and a solution is explored, and the issue taken care of."

Robin said, "I see all that you said happening in my life as a Nanny. I've gotten good at seeing a problem and finding a solution. It does make you feel more powerful, doesn't it? I see also what belonging does to those kids, too. I make them feel that they matter."

"Yep," he said. "And you always make me feel that I matter. I'm so proud of how you've grown up. And you really are a grown up. Let the validation in, please," he teased.

"Ok, ok," she said. "Now what was the other thing?"

"That's easy," he said. "Mrs. Watterson."

"Mrs. Watterson?"

"Haven't I ever talked about her? She was the mother of my playmate all those years before first grade."

Robin said, "Oh, yeah. The cookie lady?"

Gramps grew soft. "Oh, so much more than cookies. She had been a first grade teacher before she had Alfie, my playmate. And when little Grampa showed up, she had the chance to be a teacher again. Her house was my oasis from the boarding house, that one where there were no books, no music, not much of anything except work and money anxiety.

"She read to Alfie and me, every day. She sat in the middle, one of us on each side. She had an easel, and we each painted, one day a week. She had four nails, and each of our wet paintings got hung up. She made paste out of flour and water, and we cut things out of magazines and made collages. My mother never allowed anything that made a mess. There were blocks, and we built and we built. And she had a record player, put music on and the three of us danced little circle dances, so that later on in kindergarten, when the teacher said, 'I want to teach you all a little dance,' I was the first one up with my hands out on either side, ready to dance. So imagine, all the validations, all the encouragements Mrs. Watterson brought to my life. She took us to the park and taught us how to hold a peanut for a squirrel. And this is big, each week she took us to the Carnegie Library, and I could bring books home to my house, the only books in that house.

"I had a big job to let all that joy in and yet not bring it back into the boarding house to make my mother jealous. I early learned how to play my cards right. Well, anyhow, all that Mrs. Watterson gave me, made both Alfie and me the favorites of all of our teachers. You can guess what that did for self-esteem."

Robin said, "Well, that explains a lot. But back to the cheapness."

"Oh, yeah, well, does it help to know I never got an allowance? And for the most part, bought my own clothes from maybe fifth grade on. I had a paper route. Ask some other grandfathers my age. I bet a lot of them delivered newspapers. And I was good at it, got great tips when I came to collect. All through junior high, I delivered prescriptions and stuff from the pharmacy on my bicycle. Three nights a week, from six to nine. It was twenty-five cents an hour, plus tips, and, again, I was good at charming tips out of my customers. In high school, I worked as a short order chef and then on weekends, since it was during the war, I got a job working at the Pennsylvania Railroad, night shift, unloading box cars."

"Oh, Grampa, that's hard to hear."

"Hey," he said. "It's all part of building character."

"Yep, I've heard that one from my dad. By any chance was he your son?"

21

"Yes, and I'm proud as hell of him. He's done great work with you and your sisters and brother. He picked smart, marrying your mom, too. I hope you'll be that smart."

"Well, I'm building character in the process of the search, but now back to the interview. What else do you think makes you such an adorable Cheap Grampa., besides the boarding house and Mrs. Watterson and the good fall-out from those two factors?"

"I can thank the G.I. Bill for a lot of the good things that happened after the war. Oh, by the way, I didn't have to kill anybody. I was just the age to still be in boot camp on V.J. day when the whole war ended. The Navy kept me another thirteen months working the Separation Center for the thousands of sailors coming home from the Pacific. There wouldn't have been money for college. I never would have become a teacher without the G.I. Bill.

"Let 's close this honey. I bet there's enough melodrama in here to get you into graduate school. What do you think?"

"Oh, Gramps, this has been wonderful. And I know I can ask my dad, my aunt and uncles, your other kids, what they remember about cheapness when their dad was a teacher."

Gramps threw his head back and laughed. "You better let me see what they told you. But, for background, my first teaching job paid $2,300 a year. It got a little better over the years. But the kids had an allowance that was one cent more than their age. Up until your dad, the smart alec, one day said, 'Dad, I'm fifteen years old and I can't really go out on a date with sixteen cents.' So, I said, 'I'll raise it to seventeen cents, and you go out and get a job and build some character.' Just kidding."

He had that twinkle in his eye again. "Make sure one of them tells it was years before they knew bananas were really yellow, because I always bought reduced for quick sale ones that arrived home more ready for banana bread than slicing on your cereal. Or about the trips to the famous used bakery store, the place where the kids got a 'treat' of buying the week-old glazed donuts that had lost their holes, they were so smashed, and the Danish pastries, old enough to go back to Denmark."

She laughed, and put her notebook down, and came over to him and took his face in her hands, and said, "Gramps, this was wonderful. You were just great. Please don't get rich on me and change. I like you just the way you are. But, could I possibly have three picks at the Dollar Store today?"

"Oh, I knew that was coming. Oh well, yes, you can, but only if you can still follow the old rules. You have to walk around the entire store. You can put six things into your basket, but then before we check out, you have to put three back."

"I remember the rules, silly goose. And probably only a kid who grew up like you did could have invented them. I love you, my Cheap Grampa. This interview is just what I needed."

And Grampa said, "It was just what I needed, too, Robin. It's amazing to look back, and realize the things that shaped you. Thanks, and thanks again."

ALBUM TWO
SOCIAL SCENE

Magic

Cheap Grampa was driving down the road on trash day. Always one of his most favorite days, this one had the first hints of autumn coming, the sumacs turning fire red. An even bigger joy was that in autumn, people are cleaning out stuff and holding yard sales, and that made trash day livelier than ever.

Suddenly, lo and behold, there was something on the side of the road. Autumn glory coming up. He eased the brakes to get a better look. Because a house with a real estate sign on the lawn usually means these people were moving. Beside the thing, there was a whole bunch of other stuff. Just sitting there. He couldn't believe that they didn't get around to doing a yard sale. They would have made a million bucks. "This couldn't be free junk, but I'll check, all right."

Grampa jammed on the brakes, pulled the emergency brake on, and he was out of the car and starting to look the loot over even before the engine had quit burping it's usual end-of-run burping noises.

And there, a jewel in the crown, right in the middle of the lawn, was a miracle. Maybe exactly the same year as his. Yes, he could see the name, even from twenty feet away. Magic Chef. Yes, indeedy, it was a Magic Chef kitchen stove. He raced to open the oven door. Wow. Clean as if it had just been run through the oven-cleaning drill. And those racks inside, spotless. But, now here's where you see a stove that's been neglected. He looked at the four burners and the chrome rims. Spotless. He lifted a burner, and the under pans, clean as if it were something from Martha Stewart's kitchen. "Poifecto," he mumbled to himself.

He thought of his own Magic Chef. Charred from overboiled pots, omelets that escaped from frying pans, and from experimental pies that had bubbled up and exploded in the oven.

He was glad that Grandma hadn't lived long enough to see what he had done to her Magic Chef.

It was just as the sadness inside him was growing from missing her, that all too frequent happening, when suddenly a little old lady walked out of the house. Her step was bold, and full of no-nonsense. Her hair he noticed was slightly blued.

"You like my stove, Mistah? It's a Magic Chef, you know, top of the line, and my, my, have I kept it in good shape."

"Madam, this is a regular Betty Crocker kind of stove. I can only guess the incredible meals you prepared on this stove. I think I can still smell your chicken cacciatore."

"I hardly ever used the stove."

"What, this is a barely used stove?" He pulled the oven door open. "Holy mackerel," he exclaimed, "no wonder it's so spotless."

"You won't smell no mackerels in that oven, or any other fish either. Cookies, maybe, for the grandchildren."

"Madam, this perfectly beautiful stove is a Magic Chef, and I happen to know, they are the Cadillacs of kitchen stoves."

She smiled, "Not a Cadillac, this one was a Mercedes Benz."

Then she said, "Don't admire it too much. I'll raise the price."

"Oh, I'm so sorry, Madam, I thought it was put out here because you were moving, and that I could just try and get it into my convertible and take it home, because my Magic Chef is rusting away."

"So, you thought this was for free. What, are you crazy?"

"Well, I have been accused of that. What are you asking for it, my dear? Maybe you can see how cheap I am. I may not be able to afford your barely used Mercedes Benz."

Again, she smiled her perfect-toothed smile. Cheap Grampa could not resist imagining the money she gave to some dentist so he could buy himself a big boat. "You can have it free," she said casually, fingering the lovely pearls around her neck.

"I think I hear you. You're saying, I can have it, and it's free? Lemme get this right. You spoke my favorite word in the whole English dictionary. Free?"

Without a wrinkle changing, the little old lady said, "Yes, free. You don't have to spend one single penny."

Cheap Grampa said, "I don't even care if I get a new hernia lifting it into my car. It's free!"

She said, "No problem. You'll get help lifting. My oldest son is inside. He's a weight lifter, with muscles on top of his muscles. The two of you brutes ought not to have much trouble lifting up my stove."

Grampa added, "With something free, it just keeps getting lighter and lighter."

"Well, I told the truth about it being free, not costing you one penny, but there is one condition."

"One condition? Hmm. Totally free, but with one condition? Uh, oh."

"Yes, but don't worry. It's no big deal."

Cheap Grampa sighed. "In my life's experience, 'no big deal' has always turned out to be one hell of a big deal. For example, you might mean I'd have to paint the whole kitchen where the stove used to be and not get a single drop of paint on your floor."

"No, you don't have to do no painting at all."

"You don't mean then that I have to also take the refrigerator, do you? I don't need a refrigerator and I couldn't carry it in my car anyhow."

"No, silly, my son is taking that spotless Kenmore, double door, with its built-in ice maker for his own house."

"And, now I get it, they already have a stove, a gas one, because they like cooking with gas better?"

"Oh, you're such a genius. Absolutely right. Are you always so smart and so clever?"

"Well, to tell the truth, I get that way when I'm suspicious. And this marvelous stove just keeps staring at me from its elegant position on the lawn outside your house. I wonder why you're giving it up and what is this damn condition you talk about?"

"Don't worry, old man. Breathe deeply. Quiet your old superstitions and suspicions. The Cossacks are not coming down the street to scoop you up and send you back to Siberia."

Grampa stood there with his mouth open. Trying to breathe. "You mean, you too were raised with the old Cossacks galloping down your street ready to spear babies on the end of their swords?"

She smiled, "Yes."

"What a coincidence to find such a woman with slightly blue hair who is giving me her gorgeous stove, absolutely free, with just one condition."

"Ok, here it is. Without the stove, I haven't been able to cook."

"Oh, oh, here it comes. Not one cent for the stove, but all I have to do is take you out to some restaurant, and looking at you and your gorgeous hair and perfect teeth, and pearls and all, no pizza joint would meet the condition."

"No, no, taking me to a restaurant is not the condition."

"You really had me worried there, my dear. I was suddenly thinking, I already have a stove. Not clean and sparkly like yours, but if I have to lay out dough for a fancy restaurant, it won't end up being free, at all, at all."

"Silly goose. I do want to eat, but I don't want to go out to a restaurant."

"Not even a Chinese, all-you-can-eat buffet?"

"I love Chinese, but that's not what the condition is all about."

"What, now you're telling me I have to go home and cook up something on my old stove and bring it back here so maybe you and your fancy muscled son can eat me out of house and home?"

"Goosey, you're getting sillier and sillier, but more adorable every minute. Even without a stove, I've put a delicious dinner on my table, and I was looking for some man to share it with me. It requires a special kind of man. Try thinking, a Jewish man, the likes of which it took me just three minutes to know, you are one."

"I get to keep the stove, totally free, and all I have to do is eat dinner with you, at your house, and I don't even have to leave a tip for the waitress."

"You got it. I might let you help stuff the dishwasher."

"You got a dishwasher. That's pretty fancy. When are you putting it out by the curb?"

"My daughter needs one, and she's going to get it. She gets the washer and the dryer, and me, too, after they figure a good way to wrap me up for delivery."

"Ah, so this is sort of a last supper. Is that what's going on?"

"Well, maybe the next to last supper. I have enough food for two suppers, at least, unless you eat more than I figured on."

"No worry there, lady. You probably guessed right that I'm a frugal man. I live frugally, drive a frugal car, and I eat simply, cheaply, and I only buy organic when my granddaughter is shopping with me, and it is less than twice as expensive as regular food. Get it?"

"Got it." She walked over to pat her stove, and said, "I think I knew all of that just from watching you circling this stove and the slight drool coming out of the corners of your mouth that almost became a gusher when you heard it was genuinely going to be yours free."

"Don't forget the condition. So, what's on the menu? I don't eat caviar and we're not allowed to eat chitlins, my dear."

"Well, now you know everything. I cook kosher, just like I gather your mother did."

"You gather right. And oh, it was damn good cooking. There were blintzes, brisket, chopped liver, matzo ball soup, stuffed cabbage, and what she could do with lentils and egg noodles was stuff legends are made of."

"Well, now we're talking, Mistah. Cause even without a stove, we're eating like you did when you were a kid. Come on in. I couldn't invite just any man. It had to be a man with a Russian tongue. For starters, how much sour cream do you like in your borscht? The refrigerator has a whole container. How many cubes of sugar do you like with your tea? I got an electric tea pot."

Grampa just stood there. Two tears forming, one in each eye, and he asked, "And I still get the Magic Chef, for free?"

She handed him a small napkin, smiled, and said, "Wipe your tears. For free, yes, right after the gefilte fish."

Grampa Fulfills the Condition

Her muscle-bound son came out, and almost with one hand, lifted into the back seat of the old Toyota convertible, the almost brand new Magic Chef electric kitchen stove Cheap Grampa had spotted near the curb on his cruising drive on trash day.

"Nice car you got here, Gramps. I hope the springs can hold this stove up. Do you have a derrick back home to get this exquisite Magic Chef electric stove out again?" her son asked.

"I've three neighbors, all who work in the big dairy barn next door. If they can't, I'll find three cows."

The son laughed, which was a good sign. Better than when he shook Cheap Grampa's hand, which hand hurt for a week after. "Now, I understand you're invited for dinner. A no-cooking dinner. I'll be in the back room watching football, so no funny business with my mom, do you hear?"

Grampa said, "Oh, I hear good. No problems. And I knew there was a game on today. Back at my house I have it set to tape, so I can watch when I get home. What's the score when you came out?"

"Twenty-one to fourteen," he answered.

"So, who's winning?" Grampa asked.

"Twenty-one, jerk," and he almost ran to get back inside. Cheap Grampa wondered where he had first heard that old Myron Cohen joke. Which trip to Miami? Anyhow, he walked to the door, rang the doorbell and waited. He had snagged a yellow daisy-like flower from her front garden near the curb.

"Well, look who's here. Fulfilling his condition, that's a good boy. And I see that my ever-faithful son has loaded your almost new Magic Chef kitchen stove into your car. I love convertibles. I had one, you know." Her eyes misted a little, bringing out the sky blueness in them that matched her hair. "It was a powder blue VW Beetle. I needed my son and my husband, may he rest in peace, to get the top down."

"Yeah," Grampa said. "I know Beetles. But that's another story. I brought you a flower."

"How nice of you. Did you notice I had some in my garden out front? I'm going to miss them." She put his flower right behind her left ear, and it looked beautiful.

"Thanks," she said. "Come in. I hope you're ready. You know people say, 'Sit, sit, before it gets cold.' With us, it's different, 'Sit, sit, before it gets hot.'"

"And I know why. You didn't have a stove to make anything hot, right?"

"Oh, you're so smart. Come in. This is my house. I'll give you a tour later. Come to the kitchen table. This meal ain't formal enough to use the dining room, even if we still had a dining room table there."

"It's lovely," Grampa said. "I can imagine. I look at you with the flower in your hair and I can imagine what a lovely house you must have maintained, vacuuming, and scrubbing, polishing, dusting."

"No, not me. You got me wrong. I didn't mind dust and schmutz on the rugs. Me and Artie, we went to meetings and to rallies, folk music festivals and theater. To hell with vacuuming."

Gramps smiled, and said, "My imagination has been wrong before. But now I imagine we'll have lots to talk about. I was a little worried. I'm not good at small talk. But, meetings and rallies, folk music and theater. Now I can talk."

"I gathered that about you. I'm a gatherer, and I could tell. I was at the March on Washington. Martin's big speech event. I heard Joan Baez sing. I got pictures I took that time I was there."

Grampa burst into song. "We shall overcome.... I don't want to brag, but I was a Freedom Rider, and it wasn't in no VW convertible we rode. I got pictures, too. Not pretty ones."

She took him by the hand, then, and led him to his seat. "Sit, sit, before it gets hot."

He did and he was dazzled by the display of food. It was almost in patriotic colors. The red, red borscht, the white, white gefilte fish, and he swore that was blue cheese, next to the pumpernickel bread.

Waving a finger at him, she said, "Don't tell me 'You shouldn't have gone to this much trouble.' What did I do, I opened a jar of borscht, and another jar of gefilte fish, and tore off the wrappers on some bread and cream cheese. It's dinner. Now tell me about the bridge leading into Montgomery."

And talk Cheap Grampa did, and she talked, and he asked questions about her on the Mall in Washington. And she asked questions about when he was the faculty advisor to the Civil Rights Club, whose five hundred members tutored kids in the New York City ghetto. She talked about how just last week she had been in Florida for a march for the Immokalee tomato pickers. All they were asking for was one cent more a pound for the tomatoes they picked, and for a tent with some shade for when they got a break, and guaranteed good water to drink in that heat.

The talk was what both of them had wanted. No first date stumbling, awkwardness. Cheap Grampa wasn't quite sure it was a date, but he ate all that was on his plate, and didn't want the evening to end.

"That was delicious, my dear. You are a miracle worker, not having a stove and all. But, dessert is on me."

"What, you're going to make ice cream right here in my old kitchen?"

"No, but just before I saw your stove sitting there so regally by the curb, I had dropped in on my favorite store. And they just happened to have Newman's Own Fig Newtons being offered at a ridiculously low price. Almost giving them away.
I could not resist. I bought four packages and I will walk out to my car and bring one into you."

She fluttered her eyelashes, trembled ever so suggestively, and said, "Newman's Own Fig Newtons ? I love them. I buy them even if they are $4.50 a package. I love Newman's Own Fig Newtons."

"Bet that's just as much as I have loved your dinner, my dear. Wait right here. I also stopped by my favorite orchard where they just happened to have some peaches that had dropped. It's a buy one, get two free orchard. And I did. Working together we will have cut peaches and Newman's Fig Newtons with nice hot tea and sugar cubes for our first dessert together."

She blushed slightly. "You mean there may be more desserts coming for the two of us?"

Cheap Grampa blushed a little, also, and said, "And cheap ones, too. Just you wait and see."

Grampa Gets Help On a Personal

Robin, the granddaughter, arrived for a visit, thrilling Cheap Grampa. It meant a slew of joint bike rides on the bike path where they'd do their routine rounding up of trash, rescuing little fuzzy wiggly worms, making sure they didn't make road kill out of them, and collecting bottles and cans to recycle for money.

On the trail they always marveled at every new discovery. They talked together, and really looked at things. She loved dogs and always stopped long enough to admire them and talk to the owners. He wasted time imagining how much money it cost to buy the dog food, get the shots and pay for the leashes and worm medicines. Even with their differences, they got along so well.

One day during the visit, they took a ride out to the river, one of their favorite jaunts. They leaned against the rail, watching some boats come up and go under the bridge. They waved at two kayakers going down stream.

She said, "Gramps, Mom told me you're looking for some female companionship."

"What, she thinks I think you're not a good enough bike rider?"

"Don't get smart. We're buddies. You need some female companionship your age, someone nice to take to restaurants and go out on dates, movies, and things."

"You know I don't go to restaurants. What are you trying to do, ruin me?

"Stop it before I have to say, 'shut up.'"

"Ok, I'll be a good boy. And your mom is right. I told her I'm getting ready to write a personal advertisement and put it in the newspaper. The weekly paper runs them. Costs a little, but maybe it will be worth it."

"Hey, I can help you write one. I've read a few in my life. Sometimes they can be very creative. I know yours will be, Gramps."

"Yeah, how about this. I made a few notes yesterday, waiting on the 'twelve item' line at the grocery store." He pulled out a stack of three by five cards with a rubber band around them. "It was a long line. And a few of those people had more than twelve items. I almost made a stink. Until I counted. I had eighteen, myself. Oh well."

He leafed through a few of the cards. Robin knew that three by five cards are something he never gets dressed in the morning without. He carries them in his back pocket, on the right side.

"Man seeking woman."

"Oh, that's good, Gramps. You nailed it."

"Silly goose. That's the name of the column, not my first words."

"Oh, right. I'm just excited that you're doing this. I hate seeing you looking lonely."

"That's not lonely you see. Probably hungry, or being irritated with someone on the bike trail without a helmet."

"Ok, I understand, so what did you write?"

"This is first draft, now. I'm open to suggestions for change."

"We'll see. Now read."

"Woman must not be interested in restaurants."

"That's going to be your first sentence?"

"Yeah, what's wrong with it? It fits with the second sentence. 'Must have a nice smile and no bad breath.' And I love this third sentence. 'All smokers go somewhere else. Same for alcohol.'"

"Gramps, right after the restaurant sentence, I think you've eliminated about half of the population. And if you don't say, 'An occasional glass of wine would be ok,' you'll eliminate most of the other half."

He stood up straight and looked a little officious. "Not on my property. And wait, I'm just warming up."

He found the card he wanted and read, "Woman must be willing to ride bicycles in all kinds of weather. And not need air conditioning in the summer. In winter she must be comfortable in three sweaters and earmuffs. I don't believe in heat."

Robin wagged a pointed finger at him. "There go the rest of them."

"Wait, wait," he said. "I draw some back with this next card. 'If she has to have a cat, it has to be a female cat. I would like it if she likes possums, rabbits, squirrels, mice and white rats with long tails. And would be content to watch birds at my bird feeder, over anything on TV that has commercials.'"

"Now, you're cooking Gramps. This is awesome. I like the cats part a lot. I miss our old cat, Mookie."

He flipped to another three by five card.

"Now, I say, 'Woman has to believe in social justice issues, love poetry, especially Sharon Olds and Stephen Dunn, and not feel that Billy Collins is too accessible. Instead of saying grace, I like to read a poem before meals.'"

Robin said, "I'm ok with that."

"We have to work on this next part," Grampa said. "I remember I established the no restaurants bit, but I don't think I explained it enough."

Robin interrupted, "Yeah, everyone in the family knows why. You're cheap."

Gramps looked a little wounded. "That's only part of it and you know it. The big part is I don't like restaurants because I believe in my heart of hearts that cooking together is a base line to any good relationship. I'll want to say in my advertisement: 'You will love my chicken livers, and my pickled herring and hard boiled eggs in mayonnaise dish. What's your favorite thing to make?' I'll want to ask them."

Robin took his hand. "I want to change that, slightly. That last line hints at the bad joke about women who would rather make reservations than stay home and cook."

Grampa quickly said, "Point well taken. I'll change it to 'fix' and that might draw in the Southern population, too, Texas, maybe."

"You're on a roll, buddy boy. Is there more?"

"Is there more. Texas is a big state. Ok, this card says: 'I like picnics down by the river, and for picnics I like to bring succulent rollups of provolone smothered gracefully around smoked salmon with pecans and bright dried apricots folded in.'"

"Gramps, you sound more like a cooking class. I think that may be more detail than is required in this kind of 'personal' thing."

"What, so that isn't personal enough? Look, I want to chase away as many woman as I can, so the one that can hang in through all this crap might be able to hang in with my crap for a whole evening. Oh, that reminds me, we have to add this: 'I don't do small talk, I don't play bridge or canasta, and I cry in foreign movies.'"

"There goes another forty percent of the remaining possibilities, Gramps."

"Well, this will get the rest of them, maybe, leaving one or two really gorgeous contenders: 'Must love live theater, but that does not include 'Phantom of the Opera'. And at least once a year, you must be willing to sit through seven staged readings on new plays, in one day. From 11 a.m. to 11 pm. We can eat provolone wrapped smoked salmon, pecans and bright orange dried apricots during the breaks.'"

"Gramps, I don't think even I could do that."

"What, eat that much provolone?"

"No, silly goose. Sit through seven plays. How do you keep them straight?"

"Very easy. Just get into each of them. Feel it. Bathe in its uniqueness. I guess you weren't raised on as many double features at the movies the way I was."

"Ok, so what else do you want to say to chase more of them away?"

"I know this is a delicate issue, but it has to be in there: 'No prudes need apply. I'm eighty-four, but my last love said I look sixty-four. I actually feel fifty-four. And if you can read between the lines, and are interested, I would love to talk with you on the phone before we meet. Oh, before you do call, know that I am very healthy. I'm financially independent. Not dirty rich, but very comfortable, and I plan to leave my estate to my four kids, all of whom like their Dad, me, and who are such good people, each of them, in good marriages, people who work at things that make this a better world, and who gave me marvelous grand kids who see me as their cheap but generous loving Grampa.'"

"You're right about that, Cheapo," she said as she walked to surround him in her arms. "You *are* something else. I'll have to stand by and help you beat them away from your door."

"Yeah, maybe, but I think if this ever gets printed, we'll have to beat the bushes a lot to get even one taker."

"We'll see. Maybe with a little editing, we can draw a few more candidates."

"Yeah, wise guy, what do we take out?"

"Well, for starters, I'd remove that thing about the 'Phantom of the Opera'."

"O.K., you're probably right. Maybe I could put instead, something in there about 'Unless you believe in Obama, don't call.'? Or 'unless you don't shop at Deals and Steals, buy one, get two free, don't call.'? I know. 'Don't call if I catch you with a Tea Party card in your wallet.' Or 'unless you've never carried a picket sign, don't call.' Or 'if you have even a hint of racism, or anti-Semitism, don't call. Unitarians are welcome, if you're one that can make up your mind.'"

"Grampa, are you sure you really want feminine companionship?"

"Well, at least I got you. Let's get our bikes rolling before it rains, and the river rises and washes out this bridge. Thanks for your help, darling. Now, what would be in your Personal Ad?"

"I think I'd say: 'Unless you, too, have a Cheap Grampa, and need someone to talk to about how hard it is to be with someone so cheap and stingy, don't call.'"

"Hey, I think it will sell. They just have to get my approval

41

It Hinges

A Short Play featuring Phoebe and Cheap Grampa

Cheap Grampa and his thirteen-year-old granddaughter, Phoebe, are on the phone.

G- I heard my phone ringing. I immediately hoped it was you.

P- Oh, I'm so glad you're home, Gramps. How are you doing? I only have a few minutes between Wildlife Rehabbing duties.

G- I may have to drive up there and rehab you. You work so hard.

P- You know it's fun, Grampa. But I do miss you.

G- Yeah, yeah, So when do I get the deep honor of seeing you? Phones are good, but not seeing you in living color and Salvation Army fashion statements, stinks.

P- Well, funny enough...

G- You and your funny enoughs. Coincidences, coincidences. Tell me what you want so some woodpecker can finally eat this morning.

P- I fed the woodpeckers and twenty-three other birds, and some of your favorite furry friends, too.

G- That's good. I'm always so proud of you, so ok, now ask.

P- The other kids want to get together, a semi-reunion, sort of, and you're invited.

G- I'm invited. Smell me. What a gift. My retirement calendar has a few holes. But, of course, it all hinges?

P- Is that like it all depends, Grampa?

G- Nah, hinges are bigger than depends, more complications there than mere depends.

P- But, you have to say, 'Yes,' Grampa. So much both hinges *and* depends on you.

G- See, that's just what I said. I can smell the complications, the contingency clauses. But, go deeper into the well of impossibilities, woman, what does it hinge upon?

P- Well, for one thing, you have to be there. We can't do it without you. We need your presence.

G- You mean, I have to show up with presents, all wrapped in newspaper and ribbons? Now, that really puts a squeak in the hinge, baby doll.

P- But we just can't do it without you, Gramps.

G- Then, take away the presents.

P- Everybody agreed that they'd be homemade presents. Nothing store bought.

G- Nothing from Salvation Army or the flea market, either. There'd be no surprises then. I've seen everything they've had for the last six months. I don't need nothing. I've got already everything a man could want.

P- But, these aren't presents for you, Gramps. She told us she loves the idea of homemade presents, as long as you are one of them, Grampa.

G- This 'she' creature. Not one you're rehabbing is it?

P- No. You're teasing. It's the eighty-year-old widow who thinks you're the cat's meow.

G- And that's why you're throwing this party?

P- Yes, it's for her, but it all hinges on your being there.

G- What, you setting me up? What, she's going to give me her sorority pin that night?

P- Well, that's for starters. She deserves to be happy, Grampa. We all think she was invented for you.

G- Is she patented? Did anyone ask me what I was invented for? Bargain shopping, that's my destiny. Do you really want me to be happy? Buy on clearance.

P- Dear silly goose, it's not even a question. Everyone, all of us, want you to be happy the most.

G- And so you're throwing a party for her.

P- At least she thinks it's a party for her. But, we know we're really throwing it for you, and she just happens to be guest of honor, or the hostess. You taught us all that EWTFI idea. Everybody wants to feel important. We're giving her a chance.

G- And I have to be there? I have to get dressed up? Necktie and all? And probably now, because of this need to make her feel important, I have to go get my beard trimmed and my hair cut. Do you know what that costs?

P- Grampa, I'll try to be patient here. You already have forty-two neckties. I went to your closet one day and counted them. Incidentally, there's one I'd like to borrow. One of the five blue and white striped ones.

G- Blue and white was my high school colors. I like blue and white, so you can have one. Not only that, when you get one, you get another one free.

P- Thanks so much, Grampa, and for the second free one, there's a lovely paisley tie I'm going to make into a hair twister.

G- Oh, no, does that make you a twisted sister? Well, your generosity in taking two neckties, and being so good to so many birds and other creatures, especially to me, I agree.

P- To come to the party? Oh Grampa, you made not only my day, but the whole week.

G- No, no, I just agreed that you can get two ties. I'm sitting here, and in my head, I'm adding up the cost of my coming.

P- Yeah, big deal, buster, because I know something about that haircut place. I happen to know because you took me once with you, about two years ago. Remember, the second barber gave me French curls?

G- You sure looked beautiful. That's why I go back there.

P- And because it's cheap. Amazing.

G- Includes beard, too.

P- I'll say it's cheap. It cost you ten dollars. I saw that when you pulled out the ten dollar bill.

G- And I tipped her, too.

P. Oh, I know, sport. I remember hearing the dime hit the counter.

G- Now, wait a minute, did you also see that I gave her an extra dollar bill too? The tip was a dollar and ten cents on top of the ten dollar bill. That's a lot to spend for a party. Anyhow that was three years ago. The price has gone up. See, that's what I keep telling you, my coming hinges on a lot of things, inflation being one of them.

P- I've been patient, dear, dear, sweet, sweet Cheapo. What else is on your long, long list of delaying reasons for not coming, while all the grand kids are waiting for you to say, 'Yes. Yes, I'm coming.'

G- (there is a long pause) I may not live that long.

P- (shocked) Grampa, what. Are you sick or something?

G- Well, that depends. I got this swollen ankle. I got this double vision thing. Palpitations in my mashigona, not to mention swollen glands in certain glandular places, and I lost my appetite for caviar.

P- I take it, then, that despite your debilitations, you'll be there.

G- I'll be there. How could I not come? And I want to thank you kids for going to all that trouble.

P- You're not trouble. You're just a sweet curmudgeon who is our grampa.

G- The cheap one. No presents, right?

P- Unless they're homemade. You better head down to your studio and start making one.

G- Now, I take homemade means it can be something I resurrected, or re-designed, or re-invented?

P- You've never disappointed, Gramps. Go do your thing.

G- I'll look into my vault. There must be something I can put together to surprise an eighty-year-old widow. Wow. I just remembered. A pogo stick I made out of a witches broomstick, and a spring from a 1927 Model A Ford. It's poifect.

P- It depends. You'll have to show her how to pogo.

G- Oh, I will, after she learns to ride the unicycle I made from a little kid's dump retrieved tricycle.

P- I hope the party doesn't have to be held at the hospital.

G- Yes, as I said, it hinges.

Doubt

The party that the kids threw for Cheap Grampa and the eighty-year-old widow, had been a great hit with everyone. A whole week later, Grampa couldn't call his daughter without her breaking out into uproarious laughter and shouting, "Did you see that woman on her pogo stick?"

Grampa, himself, could barely believe what she had done. With just one lesson, she let loose. Spring after spring, she went so high she almost touched a branch of one of the trees. She pogoed up and down, nearly damaging at least two Subarus calmly parked out on the road, until Grampa scooped her up in his arms, while she still hung onto the handlebars of that homemade pogo stick he had made for her as a present.

He whispered in her ear, "I had some doubts. But, now I am convinced. We will enter you into the Guinness Book of Records. No other eighty-year-old widow or non-widow could match your bouncing height or sheer endurance in all of pogo-hood."

He set her back down on her feet. She looked up into his eyes, and said, "What other doubts do you have, old man?"

"We'll talk, but today is party time. Opening presents and making music. Wait until you hear the harmony the kids do on 'My Girl.'"

Very seductively she said, "I don't have any doubts that I want to be your girl. We'll talk. Come party."

It was a Wednesday night that week that they scheduled for the "we'll talk." They met at Salvation Army, open til 9 p.m. on half-off family night. She got there earlier than Grampa and already had a shopping cart filled up with stuff, none of them with pink price tags, pink being, today, the only color that was not half off.

Grampa gave her a hug and then she reached into the shopping cart and held up a pair of very, very, very short jean shorts. "I know these would be dangerous to wear on a pogo stick day, but, for a walk on the beach, poifect." She said.

"Poifect for getting arrested. The police would have to call for crowd control if you wore those on one of my beaches in Florida. Have you no morals, woman?"

"Stuff and nonsense, it's for one of my granddaughters. All of this stuff is for one or the other of them. Incidentally, the granddaughter these are for will probably cut off another inch from these jeans. A woman born to live in high fashion."

He helped her go through the check-out line, and then they sat in the car, the convertible roof open to see the moon starting to crawl skyward. Nestling up close and cuddly, she said, "So talk, mistah, what doubts you got?"

He looked uncomfortable. "Nothing about you, babe. You're better than Greek yogurt, better than a Chinese all-you-can-eat buffet, the first corn on the cob of the season. You're better than pineapple upside-down cake."

"Alright already, enough gourmet talk. What's up?"

"It's me, " Grampa said, mumbling, his usual self assurance stumbling. "I doubt I can give up being a bachelor. It's that simple."

She said, gently, "So you think I can quit being a bachelorette? I've wrestled with it myself. You think it's easy to think about no longer being able to fly wherever I want to fly, and stay as long as I want to stay? I can take on any project I want to give my time and wisdom to. Nobody can interfere with my dreams. And as long as I'm alone, I can eat what I want to eat, when I want to eat, and not even have to eat if I don't want to."

Grampa held her hand. "Those are good. And what about sitting wherever I want to in the movies, no accommodating gestures, and having the whole bag of popcorn to myself?"

"Those are good," she said. "But I don't like riding home alone with no one to talk to about the lousy plot, the predictable ending."

He held her other hand, "I wouldn't take you to that kind of movie, silly goose. And only the very best theater, maybe more than you would want."

"I'm pleasantly insatiable," she said. "And something else not so great about being a bachelorette. Sleeping alone. No quilt in the winter feels as good as a nice warm body to hold."

He laughed. "So that's it. We have a chance to make a life, and all you can think about is someone to warm up your bed?"

She laughed. "It could be worth giving up my bachelorhood. I'd even share the popcorn, and say, 'Goodbye, doubts, hello Cheap Grampa.'"

He said, "I'm touched. And you won't try to talk me out of being cheap, or going to the flea market, rummaging in the dump, or buying lots of buy-one get-one free?"

"Nah, but only if I can bring my pogo stick."

"No doubt about it, kid." He kissed her. Right there in the Salvation Army parking lot on half-priced family Wednesday's.

,

Yogurt Aisle

Cheap Grampa had been hiding out for a couple of weeks. The weather had been lousy, and the bike path just a place to get a big wet stripe up your back as you went through puddles.

So, to use his time wisely, he had been hanging out in the shop. The head lady out at the dump had invited him to come take away some of the old, rusted hulks of bikes up there, in the hope that there might be enough good parts to put something together for some kids up at the project, kids who always looked forward to a visit from him and Phoebe when she was in town. There was usually some bike he delivered. It might have a small front tire, as well as a normal rear tire, but with brakes that worked. He would add a bell he had found, and once after he had soaked it in WD 40 for a week, it rang, if feebly.

Work in the shop made Grampa hungry, but food was running low. Yogurts were all gone, the eggs down to one, and empty milk cartons out in the recycled bin said, "Go buy me a new one." Cheap Grampa held back, not really wanting to be out in the hustle and bustle of the supermarket. He had been hiding out, waiting for the weather to change, but he noticed he was also getting lonely.

Luckily, Phoebe came to town, and after a half hour of hugs and gossip, said, "Grampa I looked in your refrigerator and there's nothing there but two unopened gefilte fish jars, and a bottle of borscht. I read the date to use by, and it looks to me like it goes back to George Bush, not junior, but the senior, kiddo."

"All right. Nag, nag. Put some things on the list. We'll go right after I fix the hole in this inner tube. Then we can deliver a bike together. The kids love it when you come, and you tell them stories about wounded pigeons and squirrels with only three legs."

"That's a deal. Here's my list. I hope you won't mind picking up these few things: gummy bears, two kinds of licorice, imitation oreo cookies, chocolate chips, and six different types of caramels, including Werthers and Nips."

"So, what can I say?" Grampa asked. "Is there any room on the list for fruits and vegetables."

She said, "I left that for your list, Gramps."

"And I say, anything not on the list we don't buy it."

She said, "Yeah, yeah, I understand, rule two thousand, three hundred and ten. There will be no impulse buying."

"Good," he said. "And rule two thousand, three hundred and eleven, no visual eating when we get the stuff into the car."

She sighed deeply, "No one knows what I have to go through with you. But, oh well, I agree."

As always, once they got to the supermarket, Grampa parked as far out in right field as he could get. They walked the three miles into the store, and Grampa headed immediately to the yogurt section. Phoebe followed but wandered through the cookie aisle for a while.

Phoebe said, "I see that we're buying yogurt first. Am I right?"

"Yes, so what alternatives amongst those lovely probiotics do you see?"

"Well, my mom likes the Greek yogurt."

Grampa said, "How much does the Greek yogurt cost, my dear? Your mom has wonderful taste, but she too seldom looks at prices."

Phoebe kneeled and read back to him. "$5.85."

"In the old days, I could buy three acres of land in Greece for $5.85."

"Gramps, these aren't the old days. Now the regular Stonyfield organic is $3.99."

"And how much is the unorganic?"

She moved to the left, and reported, "$2.99."

"Ok, decision time. Since the organic is not twice as expensive as the unorganic, you know what we do."

She put two organic plastic cups into the cart.

As that moment, a lovely lady with blue hair walked up. "Excuse me, sir. I overheard that conversation. And I want to congratulate you on teaching that wife of yours how to be a smart shopper."

Phoebe said, "Sorry, madam, I'm not his wife. I'm just his long-suffering granddaughter. And he's my precious cheap grandfather."

"Oh, my eyes are bad, but even up close, he doesn't look to be old enough to be a grandfather."

Cheap Grampa said, "I ain't no kid, I'll be ninety in no time flat."

She looked at him, winked, and said, "For a man who eats good yogurt, I can wait."

Phoebe said, "I'd write a recommendation letter for him at the drop of a gummy bear. He's a pretty neat guy. You might even say he's awesome. I already see he's checking what you have in your cart. And that could be dangerous for both of you."

The blue haired lady laughed. "For an eighty year old widow, I don't eat dangerously. You, young lady, check out these organics."

Phoebe started to giggle. "Well, you're out of his price range, for sure. But he's flexible, especially when I talk to him.

"Grampa, listen up. Ask this lady if she'd be interested in joining us some morning at the bird show, at 10 AM at the campground. My instinct says she'll come."

And he did, and she did, and we did, and the adventure began.

What Should I Do?

Cheap Grampa was over at Deals and Steals, Cheap Grampa's favorite store that sells out-of-date stuff at ridiculously low prices. One of their specialties is that you buy one bag of chips and get two free. We're talking all kinds of chips here. Taco chips, potato chips, soy chips. Cheap Grampa pretends to read a sign, in small print.

"Hey, Phoebe, look at this. Does not apply to Chippies. They are buy one get one, only."

She gives him her famous rolled eyes. He gives her his famous apology, "Boys will be boys. Which reminds me," he says to Phoebe. "I got a phone call from that blue haired one from the yogurt department. Do you remember her?"

"Of course I do. I thought to myself, 'Well, let the adventure begin.' Except I'm not quite sure she isn't one of those women who really likes restaurants, so I know that will be a problem. I almost warned her when she first appeared."

Grampa said, "And that's just what the phone call was about. One of her friends has a son and the son just opened a very, very nice restaurant and they're having a Grand Opening celebration night and she has two free tickets. She said it wouldn't cost me a cent. What would *you* do, Phoebe?"

"Silly goose, I'd go and order the most expensive thing on the menu, just for recreation."

"Good, then you go with her."

"I don't want to go with her, I want you to go with her. And I want you to have a wonderful time. Do you have to wear a tuxedo? You said it was a Grand Opening."

"You think I don't have one, don't you, smarty pants? Well I do have one I wore to my Bar Mitzvah. It's been in seventy-one years of mothballs ever since. But, anyhow, this is purely a street clothes night. So I thought I'd go in my spandex suit and my bike helmet."

"Look, Mistah, I happen to know you do not have any spandex. You've moralized enough about the people who wear them without a helmet. I'm wise to you."

"But, I ask again, help me think it through. What would *you* do?"

"I told you, I'd go and have a wonderful time. Is there something keeping you from wanting to go?"

Cheap Grampa thought a bit, and said, "I don't think I'm lonely enough to want to get involved with someone with blue hair who likes restaurants."

"It's not like you have to go steady or anything. I think it would do you good to get out and experience some of the more gracious moments of life in this century, Gramps."

"And then I start thinking about all the people who don't have enough money to eat tonight."

"You can get a doggie bag before you leave. I'd even give you permission to collect some items from some of the other people at your table, and tomorrow we can take them to some of those families you've given bikes to. Go, Grampa, have a good time."

"There's another thing."

"What other thing?" she asked.

"My teeth. I went to the dentist on Wednesday."

"Yeah, so how many cavities did you have?"

"Not a one, and my sweet hygienist gave me the Flosser of the Month Award. No bleeding gums, either. And my breath, sweet as a mountain of blooming mountain thyme." He sings a few bars. She joins in on the last line.

"So, what's the teeth problem?" Phoebe asked.

"My lower bridge has a way of lifting in the presence of cheese."

"Your what does what?"

"I told you my teeth are on wires. My lower bridge, you know, the bridge to nowhere, and honey and cheese make it a toll bridge."

Phoebe said, "Ok, buster, my mom has some teeth in a bridge, too, the result of a karate accident years ago. They, too, are on wires, and they do the same thing, and remember we eat meat. Steak sometimes hangs her teeth up."

"So what does she do, duct tape them down?"

"No, silly. That would make some trouble with scalloped potatoes. Now, I've helped her with the fix. We take a set of needle-nose pliers, put some electrician's tape around the blades, and gently, very, very gently, bend the wire just enough so that even Gouda wouldn't lift it if you asked it to."

Phoebe then finished with a big grin and said, "So, you want to know what I would do if some blue haired lady asked me to go out on a fancy restaurant date?"

"What?"

"Well, first you'd have to take me to the Salvation Army so I could get the highest heels they have, and I'd get you to buy me a half-price dress full of lace, and then I'd ask your not-quite steady if I could come too. I'd love to chaperone my sweet Grampa, the cheap one. That's what I would do, if you asked me, and you did, as I remember it, twice."

He listened to her and that's just what they did.

ALBUM THREE
FINDING TREASURES

At the Flea Market

Cheap Grampa timed it just right last week. He got to the flea market after the clouds had darkened and most of the fainthearted had rushed to pack their vans and pick-up trucks to close up shop. A couple of new sellers had left in a real rush. Newscasts had talked about a potential tornado, and certainly some serious downpours. Consequently, they left behind a mound of stuff, the sight of which sang to Cheap Grampa's heart like a mother's lullaby. "Left behind" were the words of his love song.

"Free, free. Help yourself. Free, free." Grampa grinned for a minute remembering a joke one of the grand kids had brought home from school. "See, this prisoner at the penitentiary had been digging a secret tunnel. Days and nights he worked, slowly hiding the dirt he dug out among the rose bushes. Day after day, he dug. And eventually he knew that he was under the barbed wire fence and he was done.

"He waited until sunset and finally dug the last few feet and came up and out. Right into some suburban back yard. A kid's birthday party was in progress. But he didn't care, at the top of his lungs he yelled, 'I'm free. I'm free.' And the birthday boy walked up to him and handed him a balloon, and held up four fingers, and said, 'Big deal, I'm four.'"

Cheap Grampa knew that somewhere in all this junk he would find something for that kid. He read the words again. "Free, free. Help yourself. Free, free." And there was another line under the sign. It said, "Take it all or just anything you want."

Now, that gave Grampa a pause. Of course, he would take it all. Why not? It was free. There is no bargain better than free. And free without any other obligation, that is truly a triumph. Except. And now we come to a problem. Except, Cheap Grampa was there with only his bicycle. He couldn't take it all.

The torture of that was almost unbearable as he began to see what was there. There were skis, and hiking boots, motorcycle helmets, a good bicycle, two window fans, a tripod, like for a camera, and there was a camera, too. He saw guitars, even a tuba. And the sign still said, "Take it all or just anything you want." Take it all, take it all, it started to sound like a cheer.

He sat down in an old Adirondack chair that was part of what he could take. He'd always wanted his own Adirondack chair. All the glorious stuff was there, and there he was, at the right time, before the storm came, and he could have it all, all, all, if only he could get it home.

At that moment, with thunder in the background, another old guy came up to him. "Hey, Gramps, is this your stuff?"

"Well, not exactly," Cheap Grampa said. "It didn't used to be mine, but I'm about to claim it, but I got no way except my bicycle to get it home. And oh boy, could I use this stuff. Sitting there, and right up my cheap alley."

The other old guy said, maybe too quickly, making Cheap Grampa a little suspicious, "Nothing better than free, Gramps. Maybe I could help. I just happen to have a pick-up truck. Where do you live?"

"I'm up on Skinner mountain," Cheap Grampa said.

"Hey, what a coincidence, that's on my way. Is that your bike, the one without tires, or is that part of this junk pile?"

"Yep, that's mine."

"Well this whole thing makes me feel sorry for you, Gramps. Help me load up this stuff, and we'll put your bike on top and I'll drive you home."

"I'll have to pay you something, because this is the second best thing that has happened to me all day."

"Yeah, what was the first thing?"

"Seeing that sign, of course. 'Take it all or just anything you want.'"

"I get it," the pick-up truck driver said. "Ok, let's get to work." And they loaded, and they loaded, Cheap Grampa getting more and more excited about everything he had found. There was a meat grinder, and a saxophone, and two old telephones that looked like antiques, there was a monopoly game, and two old coffee pots.

The stuff fit into the truck. The pick-up guy left off one bike, about twenty years newer than Cheap Grampa's. "There, I guess we got it all loaded, Gramps." He started up the pick-up truck, the stuff rattled, and settled down, and he said, "Really Gramps, all you truly needed was a better bike, and now you have one."

He slipped into first gear and started to pull away, and he waved at Gramps. "Think about it, old man. My guess is you already have all you need." And the pick-up accelerated, and Grampa saw his old bike and he saw the new one, and he sat down on the ground and started to get into a pity-pot.

Out loud, he said, "What a tragedy. The darkest day of my life. Worse than when all the needles fell off the Christmas tree on Christmas Eve. Worse than when the dog got a nose full of porcupine quills."

Tragedies like an old movie kept projecting into Grampa's head. Until suddenly, what seemed like defeat was really just another victory. He had a new bike and he didn't have to worry about where all that junk was going to be stored.

As he neared his house, he saw something by the mailbox. By

gum, it was the Adirondack chair. A note was attached to it.

"Hey, Geezer. That was really my stuff. I left it to go get the bigger truck, and thinking if somebody needed a few things, it wouldn't be the end of the world.

"But I sure was glad to get back before the storm and you happened. Thanks for helping me load. Hope the bike works good and ain't that chair a classic. You got just what you needed. Live simply, until we meet again."

The note was signed, "Just another hoarding geezer."

Gramps said to himself. "Now, that's absolutely the best thing that's happened all day."

At the Dump

The town dump was clearly one of Cheap Grampa's favorite places in the whole world. It's right up there with visits to his kids and grand kids and the buy-one-get-two-free-out-of-date-goods grocery store, and even the day with the theater company that once a season does seven staged play readings, starting at 11 a.m. and finishing at 11 p.m.

He's on a first name basis with the woman who runs the dump. He carefully takes his recycles to the right bins, under her watchful eye, and Gramps often leaves something on the "Wall" where sometimes he, in turn, finds books, cassette tapes, and occasionally a garden tool, like a rake with a missing tooth or two.

Because he's so charming or that she feels sorry for him, she lets Cheap Grampa go up to the sacred place, way up in the back where the real loot is. It was a too hot and sticky day in August when he biked up the hill and was confronted with such a plethora of stuff that surely his bike could not handle it all. He said out loud, "Let me count the treasures." Grampa would definitely have to get back up there with the car, but in the meantime, he could stake out the finds, put one of his signs on top of them, signs he had folded in his back pocket along with a roll of duct tape.

"THESE SPECIFIC ITEMS BELONG TO CHEAP GRAMPA. PLEASE DO NOT REMOVE OR I WILL HAVE TO COME TO YOUR HOUSE AND CUT YOUR SOCIAL SECURITY CHECKS IN HALF."

First off, to his pure delight, there was a 'retired' weed eater. Grampa knew he would have fun seeing if all it needed was a clean spark plug. The sound of a so-called 'thrown out' weed eater brought back to life was music to an old two-stroke engine heart.

A real jewel was a big rubber-tired wheelbarrow, with hardly any rust, just a broken wooden handle. A delicately carved old piece of two by four, splints on either side, would make it able to roll up and down someone's driveway who needed a rubber-tired wheelbarrow. He'd fix it and find someone in need. It was Cheap Grampa's way.

Next, he untangled two sets of ski poles. Sure, it was only August, but come the first snow, there would be a teen-ager on his block, raring to go, but without poles. They were a little bent. No, they were a lot bent, but he could fix that. And attach new straps cut from an old belt where there were no straps. A piece a'cake.

Next, another piece of cake. A little tricycle, minus one wheel. Oh, a wheel was there, but crushed. Someone had ridden over it with a car or pick-up truck. But, as luck would have it, Grampa had a few wheels in his wheel department. Even if it wasn't the same size, he would get the old tricycle up and rolling for a kid he knew who needed one, badly.

Oops, and there's an ironing board for that kid's mom. He had heard her complaining. Hers wouldn't stay up. The one at the dump folded good, and when unfolded, it stood up, but the top was all burned through. Yep, he would put the two together. Her good top on top of this one, and she'd be back in business. Her business was washing and ironing. Ho, Ho, the kid could make the deliveries on his new tricycle, but he guessed he was a little young. But Gramps could maybe find a real bicycle for the older brother. Time will tell.

Grampa spotted three more things that held some promise, although his pile was getting maybe even too big for the car. One of the new possibilities was a Twirler's Baton, minus one rubber thing on the end. He remembered the washing and ironing mom saying she had been a twirler in high school. What a fun present that would be for her, and Cheap Grampa knew exactly in which bin down in his basement he had his rubber 'ends' collection. The big bin for cane tips, chair tips, and certainly at least one Baton Twirler's baton tip. Glee was spreading on Cheap Grampa's face.

Holy moly, there was an abandoned electric fan. No screen on the front, but what looks like a good blade. Looks like the same size as the fan he had found out on trash day that had a broken blade, probably why they were throwing it away. Wow. A 'poifect' fix.

Next he spotted a piece of broken plastic porch railing. The end piece. He stared at it for a long time, but nothing came to mind for a use for it. Too big to take without some focus. He sighed, a deep sigh, and took instead the bent aluminum salad bowl, big enough to have been from some restaurant or something. He'd find a use for it. Maybe for another bird feeder.

Just at that time, a guy came up with a rusted old pick up. Cheap Grampa recognized him as one of his competitors, and boy, was he glad he had got there first. It was the guy, maybe twenty years younger, who always called Cheap Grampa, 'Geezer.' And indeed those were his first words.

"Hey, Geezer, any luck today? I was planning to get here earlier 'cause I smelled you'd be here for sure."

Gramps said, "You know me and Wednesday. Even a hot sticky one like this, the treasures abound."

The pick up guy joked, "I don't see nothing 'bounding' around here except you on that old bike. Funny enough, I didn't come to get anything, but I was planning on getting rid of this bike I don't need any more. Could you use one?"

"Wow," Cheap Grampa said, "I came here hoping to find one. There's a family with an eleven year old that could really absorb one. I found a little tricycle I can fix up for the younger kid, but nothing was here for the big brother. Lemme see what you got."

The pick up guy got out of the truck. Walked around to the back, dropped the tailgate, and there it was, an old Rollfast from before the war, rusted but still red.

"You won't believe it," Grampa said. "I had one just like it when I was a kid. I worked for the butcher as his delivery 'man.' I was eight or nine that summer. Made good tips. They probably felt sorry for me. Pittsburgh is a hilly street city. I always arrived with their meat package, breathing hard. Yeah, sometimes I faked it. But the sad news was my Rollfast got stolen, right from where it was parked in front of the butcher shop and we never ever saw it again. The butcher was sorry, but that ended my career."

Pick up said, "You don't think I was the person who stole your bike, do you?"

"Nah, mine was green. Anyhow, I told you that long story so you would feel sorry for me and give this red Rollfast free."

"What, you think I'm crazy? I'll make a trade with you. What you got to trade me? Lemme look at your pile."

They walked over together, and Cheap Grampa said. "I don't think you want no Twirler's Baton, do you?"

"Nah, especially, without no rubber tip, but I like the looks of that weed eater thing. Tell you what, Geezer. You get it started up, somehow, give me a call, and because I trust you, here's the bike. Hell, it's in a lot better shape than yours."

"Yes, but mine is an heirloom. This red one I will give to a kid who will help his mother deliver the washing and ironing she does for a living."

"That's very generous of you, Geezer. And maybe she could use the baton."

"Funny, that crossed my mind."

"It's good you still have a mind, Geez. So, here's my number, and here's the bike. But, wait a minute. Say, how you gonna get it and this other junk home?"

"I'll come back with my car. It'll fit somehow."

"I like hearing how you help other people. I'm touched. I'm moved. So, put it all in my truck, and your bike, too, and I'll drive you home. Maybe you'll be able to get that weed eater started while I'm there."

Cheap Grampa reached out his hand. They shook. "You got a deal. And to sweeten the deal, I'll give you this elegant, slightly dented restaurant salad bowl."

"I'm a meat and potato man. I don't eat salad."

Grampa got in the last word. "Well, travel is broadening. Maybe I'll give you lunch when you get to my place. A little salad while I'm working on the weed eater. 'Weed Salad,' one of the specialties of the house."

Pick up guy said, "Well, we'll see. Time will tell."

"As it always does," Cheap Grampa said, getting in the last word, another one of his hobbies.

Corn

Cheap Grampa was on the way to the family reunion. Might as well call it the Corn Reunion, since corn was an absolute feature of every sit down meal at the great gala event. Corn on the cob was *the* nightly ritual along with the shucking ceremony right over the compost pit. A different crew of grand kids hustled into shucking on a rotating basis. We're talking probably forty ears of corn every night.

At least one morning during the bustling weekend there were corn fritters or corn pancakes depending on which part of the country the flipping chef was from, and that was rotated, too. Vermonters tended to frit and the New York State leaned on pancake. Cold versions of both were sometimes late-night snack food.

And corn was cut up into the nightly Salsa along with the usual peppers and cukes, onions, etc. that brightened both ends of the long groaning boards that made up the table where the eighteen people sat to feast every night.

As fate would have it, Grampa got a call one morning that said the chef had nominated El Cheapo to go pick up the night's corn on his way over to the reunion. Right then and there a deep moral conflict developed in the old geezer. He knew who the official designated corn lady was. The one who held her regal throne over the most expensive corn in the entire valley. And just like it was with ice cream, the spoiled brats he called his family demanded they had to have the best. It still burned in his stomach when he remembered figuring out how much those many flavored hand-dipped quarts of gourmet ice cream would add up to if you multiplied that into half gallons, the cheap kind of ice cream Cheap Grampa bought, so readily available as a buy-one-get-one at the local super markets, even if they no longer contained sixty-four ounces, they cost about a tenth of that other stuff.

So, that afternoon there was Cheap Grampa's problem. Each of the supermarkets was on Cheap Grampa's way to the party, just one easy drop off, right next to the highway. And they were both using corn as one of those mouth-watering enticements to come in and shop their corn and more. Corn was this week's big loss leader, as it were. Buy corn cheap and stay to shop some more.

One store had it six for $1.00. And the other $2.25 a dozen. Both bragged that it was local corn. One of them even told you the name of the Polish farmer down in South Hadley. Local really meant local to that market.

But the legendary corn lady of Whately never had her corn on sale. The very first ears were $6.00 a dozen, and way until the last ear was picked it would still be $6.00 a dozen which made it Cheap Grampa's dilemma. There were deeply held principles in this heartfelt struggle. To buy something three times as expensive almost made Cheap Grampa ride down the center line of Interstate 91, as he wrestled with his morals.

"Hell, they wouldn't know the difference. Corn is corn. Or maybe I could confuse them. I could buy one dozen of the corn lady's and three dozens of the $2.00 a dozen super market variety. Mix them up. They'd never know the difference. I would bet on it."

Well, the way highways work, Cheap Grampa missed the exit to the supermarket and had to get off where the corn lady's castle was. He drove up, and her first words were:

"Hey, haven't seen you. Where you been? I've wanted to tell you that the floor mat you gave me a month ago so my feet wouldn't hurt, after you heard me complaining, has been perfect. It's made all the difference in my life. And because of that, just for you, Gramps, my price today is $2.00 a dozen. Do you need the usual four dozen they always buy for reunion? That'll be eight bucks. And thanks again, Gramps, you sure know the way to a lady's feet."

He handed her eight sweaty dollar bills, and said to her, "You don't know what a difference you made to *my* life today. Thanks, Corn Lady. Thanks."

As he drove off, happy with his bargain, even happier that he did not have to lie, Cheap Grampa knew that tonight he would eat three ears of the best, most expensive, cheap corn in the valley.

The Bird Feeder

Cheap Grampa went up to visit his daughter and her family living in Vermont.

He kept under 50 mph, to save gas, "My God, I could have driven to California and back in the old days for what gas costs today just to get to Vermont."

But, he'd do anything for that family, which includes the son-in-law, the soon to be on the New York Times Best-Seller-list-novelist, and the awesome thirteen year old Bird Woman of Vermont, that kid helping out the region's most respected birds and small mammals rehabilitation expert.

At last count they told Gramps there were twenty-two birds and eight mammals in many cages in various parts of the Vermont house. It would be another feathered adventure for sure. During the last visit, for some reason, a pigeon, or something, kept landing on his head when he was wearing his "Don't Forget My Senior Discount" baseball hat.

When Cheap Grampa finally arrived at their house, and after all the hugs were deeply registered and he had taken a solid tour that introduced him to each of the cages and the baby squirrel nursery, he went out to sit under a tree. He looked at the lovely mountains all the way into New York State to the west, and to the east, he spied the Green Mountains so loved by his Vermonters.

Looking up into the tree, Gramps saw that from a branch there hung a bird feeder. Oh well, if the birds didn't make too much noise, he thought he would catch a nap before the dinner his marvelous daughter was preparing, the smells wafting out of the kitchen already increasing his creativity and cheapness.

But their elaborate three-tubed bird feeder kept staring down at him. He saw how the birds loved it. At one time he spotted four goldfinches feeding in a noisy party. His granddaughter, the great shopper at the Salvation Army on Half Off Family Wednesday's, told Gramps that they had paid the full retail price of $29.95 for that feeder, words that drove Cheap Grampa into action. The nap would come later.

"We can build something for nothing," he said, and taking his granddaughter's hand, and telling her mom, "we're off on an adventure, but we'll be back in time for dinner," they went to his car, got it started up, shaking the way it always shook, and off they went to the town dump. They hadn't been there five minutes, scanning the joint, and low and behold, there was a six foot piece of poly pipe, maybe a little big at three inches in diameter, but cut into three pieces, each two feet long, Gramps said, "I almost got us a bird feeder, my darling bird girl."

She was always good at helping design things, so she started with, "But, ok, we got tubes, maybe, but how do the birds eat through the tubes to get to the bird seed?"

"Oh, golly gee, did you remember I never travel without my drill? We will make holes. Big holes for the lovely sunflower seeds the cardinals like, and smaller holes for the mixed seeds the chickadees devour."

"Right, Gramps, and a smaller hole yet for the little black seeds the goldfinches adore?"

"Right. And look, look, over there, an old pie plate with a bent rim. With my supply of baling wire, it will make a 'poifect' tray for collecting knocked out seeds."

She smiled. "Poifect it is, Gramps. But, what about the squirrels? Nice open tops on your drilled pipes, three inches wide. The squirrels will move right in."

"Ho, ho," he said, "You think I haven't thought about bird feeders' prime enemy? Those things should be out collecting acorns for the winter. I'll just lace barbed wire over the top."

She rose to her full thirteen-year-old height, and said, with a humph in her voice, "You anti-animal lover. I cannot stand by and see such cruelty. Have I not taught you anything?"

"Oh, you sound like me. I was just kidding. We'll find something even bigger than the pie plate for the roof. Ho ho, do you, can you, possibly see that roaster lid, over there?" He pointed in the direction of a torn beach umbrella. "That lid even has a handle, by which we will hang our bird feeder, making use of that beach umbrella's handle, as well. So our bird feeder is equipped with a cover of beautiful, blue enameled steel, as if someone had just discovered a way to make a bird feeder squirrel proof."

She said, "Well, all I can say is 'We'll see. Time will tell.' But, whew, you had me scared before. I knew you were better stuff than that barbed wire gag."

"I am better than that, but the lid will not keep the squirrels away really, but lo and behold, do you see it? Way over in the north of the dump, someone has thrown out some metal fencing material. Little one inch squares. Can you picture it, wrapped around our pipes, holding them together? With little blocks to make room for the finchy winchy's and the chick, chick chickadees."

"But no squirrels. Oh, Gramps, you're a genius. Let's get out of here before the bears eat us. I'm eager to get to work on making our genuine, artificial three-tubed bird feeder."

They left, but not with a humph, just full of the joyfulness the two of them always had together.

It didn't take them long to get it all assembled, and they invented together something to make it easy to get the roaster lid off and back on again. They also found some bamboo tomato stakes that they cut and drilled holes in to give the birdies something to stand on in front of the holes, at just the right height, a height that was determined by the Bird Woman, who knew how to make it perfect even for littler fledglings.

"Well, it's a beauty Gramps. Now, let's get to the farm store and buy the three kinds of seed you'll need."

That announcement was received in utter silence. Bird woman waited. "What's wrong, Gramps? You've turned quiet."

"What? I have to buy seed? Spend money on birds who should find their own seeds? You mean, if you're a bird feeder person, you have to buy seeds?"

"I don't know any other way, Gramps. We always have to buy seeds, and sometimes, when money is short, the feeder remains pretty empty."

"Stop me if I'm wrong. Are those sun flowers growing out there, decorating your garden?"

"Hey, you're right, we can experiment with some of their seeds, Gramps."

"At least it's a start. Let's go and see what else." They held hands and walked out to the garden. "Ho, ho, do I happen to see a squash that some clumsy person harvesting in your garden just happened to step on. And do you, without blaming anyone, maybe even thanking them later, see that there are visible seeds small enough to put into torpedo tube #2?"

"I do, I do, Gramps. And suddenly, I just remembered Mom groaning about some old flower seeds she found, out in the garage, with an out of date thing on the package that said, 'Use before Sept. 2008'"

Grampa picked her up, twirled her around the garden twice and said, "Ok, genius, we're off to the garage. You grab the squash and with my handy only slightly rusted Swiss army knife I will cut us a used sunflower. I think we're in the bird feeder business."

She put her hands on her hips, and looked at him. "You have to add, Gramps, we're in the 'cheap' bird feeding business."

"So, what's new? With me, how could there be any other way?"

ALBUM FOUR
BIKE ADVENTURES

Library

Cheap Grampa told Phoebe, "You may think this is the end of our bike ride, but I ain't ready to go home yet. Look, I do believe that's a library I see, and I'm the kind of guy who loves looking into libraries. I also know it's a library where they know your grandma and you."

It was a lovely little building, lots of windows, and beautiful flowers all around it. It was way out in the country. Grampa said, "You wouldn't think it would reek of sophistication and up-to-date hood." Phoebe was anxious about going in and trying to take out books without a card, especially after Grampa acknowledged that he didn't have a card either.

"I'll just come back with my grandma," she said.

"Nah," Cheap Grampa said. "I've been conning librarians all my life, particularly when I had a book still out that was due a year ago. I'm sure they know your grandma, and we'll blame the fact that you didn't bring your card on the fact that you were chased by a coyote when you were out walking your dog, and in the sheer terror of it, you forgot to bring the dumb card."

"Now, Grampa, I don't mean to lecture you, but that would be a bold faced lie. I really am on a mission with you. The truth always works," she said, from a position as lofty as Mount Kilimanjaro.

"What, even in the presence of a brand new round tin of chocolate covered cashews? Or a tall can of honey-dipped almonds? Or a bag of delicately frosted walnuts?"

She smiled that lovely wide toothed grin. "Well, it would depend if those nutty nuts were in a closed closet, where I could not see them. I have this visual eating problem you have pointed out to me. Oh, and that closet might have to have a hasp and a padlock on it, and I might not happen to know where the key to the padlock happened to be."

"Honorable right down to starvation. All right already, we're at the library. Let's go in and see how many Danielle Steel novels you haven't already read."

As we walked in, the librarian indicated that she recognized Phoebe, if not by name. She said, "Nice to see you back again. You're the kid who's into animals, aren't you? How's your grandma? She hasn't been in for a while, either."

"Oh, hi. Grammie gets real busy when I get down here. I usually travel with a lot of creatures, and she always pitches in with some of the care."

"You travel with animals? What, a dog or two?"

"Well, not exactly. We only have one dog, but..."

Cheap Grampa interrupted. "The but is a very long but. Would you believe it? But nine cats, but two possums, but three rabbits and birds. Has she got 'boids,' you might ask? I'll tell you. She has twenty-two birds, and all twenty-two birds are in need of the whole family's attention, and furthermore birds ain't cheap, I'm here to tell you."

Phoebe interrupted him. "My Grampa exaggerates a little. I am working with an Animal Rehabilitation person, and I sort of help her out. My generous grampa here, with all of his grumbling, has helped us a lot, too. He put up some of the money to pay for the big cage that has been a real godsend."

The librarian looked at Grampa, and said, "I had one just like him. My grampa was always grumbling, but sweet as a bunch of lilacs in April. You know something? There was a time in my life when I kept finding birds that had fallen from nests, and some that cats had caught and didn't kill, just abandoned. Once I became the librarian, I didn't have time for that. I guess I'm just healing books in the back room now. But, I just remembered. I have a couple of cages I hope you could use."

"What a lovely offer," Grampa said. "Like could we check them out, and have a library card that says they're due back in two years or so?"

She laughed, a louder laugh than is usually allowed in a library. "These come with a three year check out, and it's renewable for life. Did you come by car? I've been storing them in the basement here at the library."

"Who needs a car? We came on bikes, but I got bungee cords. We can just bungee them to our bikes. Unless your cages are cougar and panther sized. Are they?"

"No, just birdcage sized," she said.

"Well, lucky us, we found a lady in a gilded cage, Phoebe. Generous as the whole State of Massachusetts."

Phoebe and the lady went down to the library's basement. When they came up, they dusted off the two cages. Grampa said, "We can manage these just fine with our bungees. But, if you happen to hear a loud metallic noise outside, don't worry. It was just us dropping a cage or two on the highway."

"Oh, Grampa. You're a silly goose."

"These cages are for 'boids', not a gaggle of geese."

Phoebe rolled her eyes, shook hands with the librarian, and said, "Thank you so very much. We really need them, and these are wonderful."

"My pleasure. And you two are pretty wonderful as well. See you in three years, or sooner if you can find some time for books. That will make me feel lucky."

Grampa, Phoebe and the Smoker

Cheap Grampa and Phoebe, the thirteen-year-old granddaughter, were standing on the bike trail bridge that went over the Connecticut River. It was that time of year when the crew teams from the colleges in the area were out practicing in their sleek, long shells. Phoebe and Grampa could hear the coxswains calling out, "Stroke, stroke."

Another biker pulled up alongside them. Leaned his bike against the rail and fished out a pack of cigarettes and lit one up. "Used to do that kind of thing when I was in college." he said. "Our team won the Eastern Conference Championship in my senior year."

Phoebe said, "Wow, that was quite an accomplishment."

Grampa said, "Were you smoking back then?" Phoebe got nervous. Grampa was going to nail that guy, and there might be trouble ahead.

"Of course not. We were conditioned strenuously. It would have been unthinkable."

Grampa softened. "So, when did it change?"

The guy said, "I don't take to being preached at."

"I don't preach, but I like asking questions. For example, I see a mother riding on the bike trail. She has a kid, but there's no helmet on her. So I ask, 'If you get into an accident and die because you didn't have a helmet on, who's going to raise your kid?'"

"That sounds preachy to me."

"But you wear a helmet. I saw it when you pulled up. Here's

another question. How come you wear a helmet?"

The man laughed, "I can see the curve ball coming. Strike one. Yeah, I know you. I wear a helmet because I want to live."

The three of them stood there silent for a while, watching the racing shells glide under the bridge.

Grampa said, "I have another question. Do any guys your age do that kind of rowing now?"

"Oh, yeah. There's a big Master's category, people fifty and over. Almost every river that isn't overrun by motorboats has a club or two, and races are held all through the summer months. And I'll answer the question I know is forming under that gray head nestled into that red helmet.

"I'm just standing here, taking a smoking break, but you're smart, we both know the answer is that I can't join in because of the smoking. I just wouldn't have the wind or the endurance that's needed, and I don't like you reminding me."

Grampa said, "From the very topic, you must see I meant you no harm. Maybe a little discomfort, but what I asked you comes from a good heart. What, I should see a handsome guy like you killing himself softly, and not mention it?"

"Ok, I've tried to quit, joined groups, read up on what other people say about how they broke the addiction, and addiction is what it really is. I tried, but had no luck with the patch. You addicted to anything, Mister?"

Phoebe said, "He's addicted to being cheap, but he's delightfully inconsistent. He won't buy expensive ice cream. He never takes us to restaurants. He bikes every errand instead of taking the car, and then gets us a really good bike, or a camera if he sees we're ready for it. Some of us grand kids think it's just an act he puts on. He's cheap, but so generous, it ruins his reputation all the time."

"You love the guy, don't you?"

"We all do. He's contagious in a way. We all feel like better human beings when we've been around him a while."

"Thank you, darling, remind me to up your birthday bucks to two dollars for every year of your age at your birthday party."

"You two are really sweet," the smoker said as he snuffed the cigarette out on the iron rail, and put the butt in his pocket.

Phoebe said, "I'm glad you did that. I've seen too many smokers just toss them into the river."

"I used to do that," he said.

Phoebe now rushed in with a question, "What made you change?"

"I see your Grampa's contagion, now that you start with the questions. Good for you. Well I met a woman. And I fell hook, line and sinker for her. Her name was Grace, a genuine environmentalist with a capital 'E'. She was at the first Earth Day March, and she's kept doing green things ever since."

"I'm like that, too. My Grampa helped train me. Look in his basket. We always go out with two bags. One we use for the rounded up beer cans and plastic bottles. He lets us keep the money when we turn those things in. And there's another bag for actual trash. It's amazing what people toss out of their cars."

Grampa asked, "You said, 'her name *was* Grace?"

"She died. A year ago. Are you ready, big questioner? She died from lung cancer, although she never smoked. She died in my arms. I had quit, because of Grace, for the whole last month of her life."

Phoebe said, "If you were my uncle, I'd be so proud of you."

"Thanks. I'd feel proud of me, too, if I had been able to stay away from the cigarettes after she died."

"Did Grace try to help you quit?"

"Of course she did. She was the poster child for being pro-active."

Phoebe said, "I'm really sorry, mister. Maybe if she hadn't died...?'

Grampa said, "And you're alive."

"Is that a question?" the smoker asked. "Anyhow, so what? Grace is dead."

"Maybe you could help Phoebe and me later today. We're going to set up a card table right here on the bridge. I picked up a dozen bike helmets very, very cheap. Phoebe and I are going to try and stop mothers who don't have one, and see if they'll take one of ours, free of charge."

The biker smiled. "Hell, that's a bargain no one could refuse."

Phoebe said, "But they do refuse."

"How can they refuse? What do they say?"

"Some say, 'I don't ride in traffic.'"

The smoker said, "That's stupid; I know they have to cross five or six sometimes very busy streets to get to the other side of the bike path. There's no logic to it."

Grampa said, "Some laugh and say, 'I don't want to get helmet hair.'"

Phoebe said, "Grampa sometimes tells them, 'Blood isn't too good for hair either.' But most of them are so defensive they don't even get the humor. And Gramps sure can be funny. He wears a turtle neck, and he's apt to pull it up over his head and walk around, moaning, 'I lost my head on the bike trail, all because of vanity.'"

The smoker said, "And I bet a lot of them pretend it only will happen to other people, not them. Damn, it's just like smokers. Only smokers also get uppity, and say, 'No one's going to tell me what to do.'"

"We've heard a lot of people who say, 'No one's going to tell me to wear a helmet.'"

"Hey, my name's Mike. What time do you want me back here to help?"

"Please to meet you, Mike. We'll be here right after lunch. Say, we brought an extra sandwich. Will you join us? We go down by the river, at the raft where the racing shells come in after practice. It's fun."

Phoebe said, "Please say yes, Mike. I know you're really going to be a help to us."

"These are cheap sandwiches, Mike. The turkey and cheese inside are all 'buy ones get ones'. Phoebe baked the bread, and I ground up the basil from our garden and made pesto we spread on the turkey and cheese."

Mike said, "I'll be honored, but on one condition."

"Yes, what condition, Mike?" Phoebe and Grampa asked together.

"Only if this will be a smoke free place for celebration."

"Your wish is our command, Mike," Grampa said.

Phoebe said, "That's awesome, Mike, and I'll see that you get the thickest sandwich, usually reserved for me. After all, everyone can give up something."

"Well, what about me, you two?" Grampa said, "Look at what I'm giving up. All those valuable helmets, totally free, not just a buy one, get one free."

Time for Helmet Day

It was a Sunday and the Island was filling up with weekend day-trippers, and more than a few locals wanting time at the beach on a day off. Cheap Grampa, in an uncharacteristic harsh voice, said to his granddaughter from up north, "Get your helmet on. Time's running out."

"What's up, you old grump? An alligator biting your tail?"

He didn't bother to be sarcastic about her wiseacre remark. "Not only your helmet, but this card table, too. I'll bring the signs."

She looked at him with a puzzled expression. "What signs? Why do we need a card table? And if we're going to the beach, as planned, Grampa, how am I going to carry it on my bike, anyhow? Oh, wait, Phoebe, you already know the answer to that question. It's going to be bungeed to my back, and become just another example of grandparent abuse. I'm gonna report you."

He laughed his rather shallow laugh, the one he used to acknowledge someone else's joke. It was a laugh he would never tolerate for one of his own jokes. She knew that, and she knew she had hit the bull's eye.

"As a matter of fact, that's just right. Now bungee your mouth shut while I go get the helmet box." A minute later, out the door he came, with a box that barely fit through the door, and was about as tall as a deluxe refrigerator.

"Oh, sure I get it. It's helmet day, right?"

"Right you are, buddy girl, and time, as I said, is running out, out, out."

"But Gramps does it have to be on the day before I fly back up north? I was hoping we could swim all day."

"The water's full of manta rays. There's no swimming. The beach is closed."

She gave him the famous look. "I know a bald faced lie when I see one. Show it to me in the newspaper. 'The beach is closed.'" Hands on hips, she humphed, "Yeah, I bet."

"It won't be in the newspaper. The chamber of commerce never lets them put in the paper shark attacks or manta ray stingerinos. But you got me. Ok, I lied. And we *will* get to the beach. In fact, we'll set up right on the bike path leading to the beach. A poifect place."

"Yeah," Phoebe said. "A poifect place for you to play Messiah and shame everyone who is not wearing a helmet."

Grampa pretended to be hurt. "You are protesting my missionary work? Well, it won't be on my conscience when someone we could have saved ends up as road kill on this Island because she didn't wear a helmet." Then he went into his syrupy voice, the same one she has learned to use when she needs twenty-five cans of Wellness Brand cat food, the expensive one, for her zoo up north.

"But, honey," he purred, " I'm only asking for an hour of your beach time. We'll set the egg timer. Flip it, and one hour later, when the sands of time run out...." His voice became a whisper as his eyes glazed over.

"Oh, don't go poetic on me, Grampa. I agree. I believe in helmets, and you know I do. But you get one hour, in real time, time that will be timed by the timer I just happen to have right here in my pocket. That sand in your old egg timer is so old, days could pass before three minutes would ever be up."

"You carry a timer, a genuine, official Beach Helmet Day timer? Smell you. No wonder I love you so much."

"Love, schmove, just tell me, Gramps. How the heck are you going to carry all those helmets?"

"No problem. Way back when I served as a water boy for the Chain Gang in Mississippi, we carried buckets of water on our shoulders, hanging them from a long stick, as I remember it."

"Well, travel is broadening. That's the first time I've heard about you spending time in Mississippi. I can picture it, even if I can't believe it. But, I have an imagination. A long stick with these buckets hanging. Get the joke? Helmets referred to as buckets."

"Brilliant, yes, you are brilliant, I get it. I got it. Now don't you get a big head just because we both think you're so smart. Ho, ho. Did you get my joke? Big head, helmets, buckets. I think the long stick will work."

She started to laugh. "Grampa, it could be your schtick for today's show." He gave her the look of utter disgust which is really the look of envy, and she knew it, but she said, "Oh, well, Carole Burnett didn't get a loud laugh every time, either."

Grampa waved a finger at it her. "This is not TV. We're not on the Ed Sullivan show. Today is Helmet Day, and your cooperation is required. This whole project will take a little coordinating. And you know I could never do this without you."

"Quit conning me. I'm already committed. But you have to promise me one thing I believe in."

"What, what? In all the thirteen years we've known each other, have I ever tried stopping you about something you believe in?"

"Well, nothing that didn't have a big price attached to it. Cheap things you support. And this is one of them. I believe that every person who takes one of your flea market helmets gets a flower to wear in his or her hair, behind her or his ear, right through the air hole on the side of the helmet."

He looked at her tenderly, and said, "I know you're a floral, moral, kind of teenager, and I respect that, but I'm not going to spend any money buying flowers."

She then rose to the full stature of her thirteen years, this is, of course, before the card table was bungeed to her, and said, "Open your eyes, blind man. You got fifty or more daisies growing right there in your front lawn."

"Don't blame me, I never planted those flowers."

"Well," she said, in her patient voice. "Birds pooping must have spread the seeds for you. I just know I'm going in to get a scissors and I'm coming out to cut thirty daisies. Your job, sir, is to get a nice can filled with a little water, and that can we will put inside a small bucket, the handle of which will hang from your Chain Gang pole from which all those helmets are going to be hanging. Did you hear me? No arguments. Flowers are the way to a woman's heart and I suspect most of these helmets are going to go to women."

"I agree, woman, and your courageous stand makes me want to make a speech." Grampa got up on his soapbox, at least his voice did, and this is what he said. "Mothers, mothers, I implore you to hear my voice. Do not go one more pedal down this bike path, or through any puddle, without a helmet. I am not here to sell you a helmet. Your commitment to live longer than your children demands that you take one of these flowers with your donated helmet for your safety."

Phoebe patted him on the back. "Nice job, Mr. President. That line about living longer than your children needs some work."

"You're right. But the main thing I want to preach at them is that if they get killed because they didn't have a helmet, who is going to raise their children? I could point at you, and ask the mothers, 'Would you want this immature thirteen year old to be your kids' mother after you die because you didn't have a helmet on?'"

She liked that idea, and added, "And I could point at you, and ask the question, 'Can you imagine your children being raised by this grumpy old geezer? Just imagine him at the parent teacher conference. He'd embarrass your beautiful children day after day, day after day.'"

"Oh, sweetheart, that's good, real good. It makes me so aware that you were born to the breed, because I think that will move any reluctant mother. That, and the flower for behind her ear that pokes out of the air hole in the helmet.

"Let's get going," he urged. "I'll get the flower scissors for you and the water can, and then I'll help you with your bungees. You start slipping helmets on this rake we're going to use for our pole."

Phoebe looked at the rake. It was the longest pole thing she had ever seen. "Where did you get this rake, Grampa? From Jack in the Beanstalk? You'll be wider than the bike path."

"We'll face that when we come to it. At least the helmets, if I tip the pole right, won't go off the end with the teeth. I can't wait to see who on the bike path is going to have his teeth knocked out with that rake. Well, once we get rid of all the helmets, and flowers, we won't need it any more. We can bungee it to the card table on the way home."

She turned to him, in her most grownup manner, and said. "I wear the table going, and you wear it coming home. After we all go swimming. And I just hope we get rid of all these helmets in the hour I have committed to you, Grampa."

He answered her, "It's not even a question. We have a product here no one can refuse. And besides, once the helmets are all gone, I can use the rake to scare away the manta rays. Or we can go dig up clams for supper, or rake in a couple of porpoises and when we get home grill them succulently with lots of garlic and peanut butter."

She knows how to play with him when he gets insane, so she said, "Only if I can sprinkle flowers on you before we put you on the grill, Gramps."

Another Helmet Mission

Phoebe, Cheap Grampa's granddaughter, looked up at the cloudless sky and said, "It's a perfect day for hitting the bike trail, Grampa."

"Oh, it's about time. I hate those rainy puddle- making days keeping us indoors."

"Come on, Gramps, the farmers needed the rain, and anyhow, I never mind getting a stripe up my back from going through the puddles."

"Easy for you, you don't have to worry about the rheumatism, the arthritis, and the tritaforthitis, etc, either."

She laughed, and said, "Neither do you. So put on your helmet and let's get going. But, hey, what's with the croquet mallet?"

"It's the first time I've ever brought it along. And I promise not to bop any lovely dogs we meet on the bike bath."

She gave him the look, "I certainly hope not, but I'm not sure you aren't going to bop some human beings."

"Only if they're not wearing helmets," he said with one of those twinkles and wrinkles at each eye.

"Oh, Grampa, you can teach them to wear helmets in some other way."

"Ok, Miss Smarty Pants, let's go forth and you do it your way and I'll do it my way."

"Yeah, well, who's gonna have to take you to the emergency room when some non-helmet-wearing guy beats you up for bopping him with a croquet mallet?"

He answered with a grin, "You, of course, but I'll be very discriminating and only bop grandmothers smaller than I am."

"And if they're with a grampa?" she asked.

"If he's not too macho, and not wearing a helmet, I'll bop him, too."

"Oh, this is going to be one glorious ride. I can see trouble ahead."

"I'm very discreet. And I'm just out to educate. I got some of our flyers, about the statistics of people getting killed because they didn't wear a helmet. We'll give one to everyone I bop. Will you be in charge of passing them out?"

"Grampa, I'll speak my truths here. I don't want anything to do with this bopping scene."

"What, what? You'd abandon me on a cause I thought we both believed in?"

"Now, you know I'm for bicycle helmets. I preach as loud as you, but I'm against physical violence. I'm against spanking, and you know, I'd stand up against anyone hurting any animal."

"Anyone told you how loveable, precious and dear you are?" he asked her.

"Well, not for about ten minutes, not since we started this journey and that nutty croquet mallet showed up for the first time."

"Well, you are all of those things to me, and look, I'm taking the mallet out of my basket and I'm hiding it in the bushes here. We can get it on our way back. Are you satisfied, now?"

"Yes, and has anyone told you lately how flexible you are, and precious, and dear and loveable, too?"

"It took you this long to notice? Ok, I accept. Now let's get going. Ahoy mate, I see two people on bikes approaching from the west."

"And Gramps, they're both wearing helmets. Let's stop and validate them."

"I'm already rehearsing what I want to say to them."

The two bikers came closer. It was clear they were not a young couple, but they were a couple. He was leading, and she was single-file following. Grampa spoke.

"Good morning, you two lovely helmet-wearing lovers. This is my granddaughter, Phoebe, and we're out celebrating people wearing helmets, and you are the first on this lovely, sunny, perfect bicycle riding day."

The woman spoke. "Of course, old man, we wear our helmets, even in bed."

The man said, "You can't be too safe these days." And they both laughed and Grampa and Phoebe joined in. The man got back up on the pedals and said, "We hope you find a lot of people in helmets."

Phoebe said, "It means a lot to my grandfather. You made his day. Have a great day yourselves, and if you see any folks up ahead without helmets, you might warn them that there's a fanatic on the bike path they'll have to deal with."

"Will do," the woman said and blew Grampa a kiss as she biked off.

"Well, we're winning, one to nothing." Grampa said. "Hmm, that blown kiss, maybe she's his sister. That could be nice. I like her red, white and blue helmet."

95

"Grampa, they were a couple, I could tell. She was just playful."

"Yeah, and I bet *she'd* join me when I go out with the croquet mallet."

"Hey, Grampa, look. A young couple coming our way. A very macho guy, look at those biceps, and Gramps, they're both wearing helmets."

When they got just a little bit away, Grampa swerved right into their lane. Muscle man jammed on his brakes, and so did his woman friend. Phoebe could hear the tires squealing.

"Hey, you crazy old man," macho man said with anger flaming under his helmet. "You could have caused a serious accident."

"I know," Grampa said, very calmly. "And it wouldn't be the first one out here on the bike path. I just wanted to stop and congratulate you both for wearing helmets."

She said, "With crazies like you out on the path, we sure might need 'em."

Phoebe smiled and stepped closer. "My grandfather is really dedicated to wearing helmets. And he has such trouble with people who don't wear them. He had a student who was killed because she didn't have a helmet on. I'm sorry if he almost caused an accident."

Macho man turned, and reached out his hand to Cheap Grampa. "I'm sorry for getting angry at you. I'm a teacher, too, and I'm sorry you lost one of your students. I understand. Just a couple of weeks ago a kid from my school was killed by a drunk driver. He wasn't my student, but it hurts all the same, doesn't it?" Grampa nodded his head.

Then the woman spoke. "I'm an emergency room nurse, and oh the ugly stuff I've seen come in off the bike paths, where everyone thinks you don't have to wear a helmet, because you're not out in traffic or anything. Kids keep getting knocked off their bikes by cars coming out of the shopping malls, and not even looking for anyone coming down the bike path."

Gramps then said, "Hey, you two, would you give us ten minutes? I see bikers coming our way. Four people. Probably a family. The two kids have helmets, but neither of the adults do. Will you help me while I talk to them?"

"Oh, Grampa, please no preaching."

"Who preaches, I'll just ask them a few questions. And our new friends here can tell their stories."

Phoebe said, "O.K, Gramps, but not that question that goes, 'Folks, I see you believe in helmets, and I'm happy to see the kids are wearing them. But, what plans do you have for your kids when you're killed today on the bike path because you were too stupid not to wear a helmet?'"

"Ok, honey, I promise not to say that one, or at least, not the way you satirized it. Maybe, I could really say, 'This new friend of ours is an emergency room nurse, and she knows the biggest organ donors are people who have died of head injuries because they didn't have helmets on.'"

The nursery room nurse said, "Right on Gramps. That's what we all say at the hospital."

Grampa put his arms around Phoebe, and said, "I'll be good honey. The support I'll get from the three of you will make me less crazy. But don't count on it if a mother comes down the path without a helmet and her two little kids both have helmets on. That's when I go nuts."

The two new friends, almost like a chorus, said, "We'll go nuts with you, Gramps."

97

Howl

Phoebe was excited. It was going to be a nighttime bike ride.

Earlier that afternoon, Cheap Grandpa had laid out two small flashlights on the dining room table, and two new things she hadn't seen before. They, too, were lights of some kind.

"What are these things, Grampa?"

"Do you notice the curve? And these 'hooker-oners underneath? Please bring our helmets in, will 'ya?"

"I can't go riding now. I have a piano lesson in about fifteen minutes," she said, glancing up at the big wall clock over the kitchen sink.

"Would I interrupt your brilliant career as a concert pianist? Am I someone to stifle the creativity in a granddaughter destined for greatness?" he asked in a merry tone. "I'll answer my own questions. No way. I just want to show you something related to helmets."

Phoebe came over and gave him a hug, on the way out to the garage. "Ok, I trust you. I am on my way."

When Phoebe got back with the helmets, he showed her how the new light things hooked right under the sun shade thing on the front of their helmets.

"Cool, Grampa." And it took her about half a second to find the button and turn the headlights on. "Wow, that's great. Now anyone can see us coming in the dark."

Grampa took on an ominous tone. "Ah, yes, for tonight, in the dark of the moon, we'll be able to see wherever we go, wherever we turn our heads, in search of mysteries."

"I don't want to rain on your parade, dear Grampa, but tonight is a full moon night, not a dark of the moon night. I checked it out in the newspaper this morning."

"I knew that. But until it comes up, it will be dark, and I have it written down. It will be up over the lower eastern hills at 6:55 tonight. That's almost a half hour after the sun sets. We'll need our lights on the bike trail then. And that's why we'll eat early tonight. Omelets and full moons go together, to be eaten right after gifted music teachers finish their music lessons."

"With brilliant student, right?" They both laughed, and Grampa went off to get the bikes ready for their adventure. He heard the piano music begin in the background, and said to himself. "Carnegie Hall. I can see it."

****

"This bike trail is really dark, Grampa."

"Of course, Phoebe. That will make the moon even brighter. And we got lights."

They came to the bridge that went over the river. It was always one of their favorite places. Grampa had bungeed two beach chairs to the back of his bike. They parked, set up the beach chairs, turned off all the bike lights, and hung their helmets from their handlebars.

"What's with us stopping here and sitting in chairs, Grampa?"

"We're here to howl at the moon. I can barely wait for the full moon to howl at."

"I'm ready, Gramps. I love howling at full moons with you, but I also remembered the full moon is the only time you eat ice cream in a month."

"Howling first, and maybe ice cream later. You can practice, but no real howling until the moon comes up over the hill out there in the east."

"I'm going to practice eating ice cream, too. Because there's no maybe about it. I just happened to notice that small freezer bungeed into your basket. I saw it when you took off the beach chairs. I knew it. I knew you had something up your sleeve with this nighttime bike ride."

"All right. All right, already. You got me."

"And, Grampa, we can do dedications together, can't we? I love them."

"What do you think I was thinking? Two chairs, the full moon, the little freezer full of kumquat fudge ice cream, two spoons, two bowls, and full hearts. Everything perfect for dedications. Ooops, there comes Mr. Moon. Get yourself ready to give it one great big look. And one big howl."

And they did. Some dog answered with a howl of its own.

"Wow, did you hear that. And that moon. It doesn't waste time once it starts up, does it?"

"No, and if it hits a cloud, it just stays under for a while, and then, 'shine, shine, shine on harvest moon.'"

They broke into song together, and as they harmonized on the last note, a young couple biked up with a daughter, about six years old. Phoebe looked at Grampa knowingly; she was glad this family was wearing bike helmets so that there would be no confrontation coming from her helmet-crazy Grampa.

The little girl spoke. "Hi. Gee, I liked your singing. We could hear it way over the river. This is my first night bike ride, and my first full moon. Oh, look, look, I see it. It's so beautiful. Can you see it?"

Grampa and Phoebe nodded.

The mother said, "I'm Betty, and this is my husband, Paul. Our daughter is Carrie."

The little girl asked, "What's your name?"

Phoebe answered. "They call me Phoebe and everyone calls him Gramps, because that's what he is. Nice to meet you. We're here to eat some ice cream and howl at the moon."

Paul, the father, said, "That's some coincidence. Our family came out to howl at the moon, too."

Grampa said, "How about if we all howl together? And after some good howling, you can share ice cream with us. You seem like our kind of people. I knew it the minute I saw the helmets."

Phoebe added, "And I knew it the minute you told us you liked our singing."

The mother said, "Oh, I wouldn't want to butt into your ice cream time."

The little girl said, "I wouldn't mind butting in, Mommy."

Grampa said, "We really did invite you. And there is more than enough. The flavor is kumquat fudge."

"I love fudge. Fudge is my favorite. Please, say yes! Mommy? Daddy?"

Phoebe gave up her chair to the mother. Carrie sat in her momma's lap, and Paul sat on his gloves, saying, "I'm just fine."

"And we'll all howl together after some ice cream," Grampa said, as he pulled out a scooper from the little freezer chest and a round half-gallon of ice cream, along with the bowls and spoons. "I was kidding about kumquat fudge. Sorry, Carrie. So far, we haven't found any place where they make kumquat fudge. This is good old-fashioned Neopolitan. So you can have chocolate, vanilla, or strawberry."

Carrie said, without any embarrassment, "I'd like all three please."

Her mom rolled her eyes, and her dad said, "Nice going, Carrie." And he added, "I'll have what she ordered."

Mom laughed and said, "Me, too."

"Guess what, Grampa?" Phoebe said.

"Well, that makes five of us," Grampa said.

Phoebe said, "Hold your eating for just a minute, Carrie, because we do something special before we eat ice cream in our family. Do you want to tell them, Grampa?"

"No, honey, you're doing great. You explain. I'll get paper napkins."

"Well, this is what we do on the full moon, with ice cream. We each get some on a spoon, and maybe I'll go first, and then Grampa can go second. I make a dedication. It's to something that matters. Oh, and after the dedication, we eat our spoonful. It's sort of like a toast.

"Here goes. I dedicate this spoonful to everyone working to protect wild animals around the world."

"Me, too," Carrie said. "And now can I eat my spoonful?"

"You sure can," Grampa said. "And then it's my turn."

Phoebe said to Carrie, very gently, "One spoonful at a time,

Carrie. You have to wait for my grampa's dedication. And then you can eat your second one. It makes it last longer. Do you get it?"

"I got it," Carrie said, and waited.

"I'll go fast," Grampa said. "I dedicate this spoonful to teenagers like Phoebe, here, who devote hours to rescuing and rehabbing hurt squirrels, rabbits, birds of all kinds, and anything else that has been hit by a car, or attacked by a predator, or..."

"Thanks, Grampa, that's enough for now. Our ice cream is melting."

Paul, said, "I drink to what you said, Grampa. I mean, I eat to what you said." Everyone laughed.

"And now it's your turn, Paul. Anything at all that you want to dedicate to. Get your spoonfuls ready, folks."

Paul looked a little shy, for just a moment, and then he said, "I dedicate this one to all the kindergarten teachers in this world, and Betty, in my opinion, is the best of them."

Carrie said, "She's my teacher, too, and all the kids just love her. But I'm the luckiest. I go home with her."

They dipped in and got another spoonful. Betty held hers out. "I dedicate this to all the doctors who work in emergency rooms of hospitals around the world. That's what Paul does, and his stories could curl your hair. But tonight, just curl your tongue around this kumquat fudge."

They laughed, and with dedication after dedication, they finished the half-gallon, and took each other's addresses and emails and Facebook pages, etc.

But Carrie said, "We didn't howl. I can't go until we howl."

Phoebe laughed. "It'll sound even better with all that ice cream in us. Ok, everybody. Hands to cup your mouth, and at the count of three, we howl. You say the one, two, three, Carrie, please."

And she did, and oh, did the five of them howl. They howled so loud that a coyote howled back. They looked at each other with amazement. Paul said, "I think that's enough. We got what we came for and a whole lot more. We have to go back in that direction."

Phoebe said, "They never come after people who smell like vanilla, chocolate and strawberry."

And it was Betty who said, "We will surely plan to be at this bridge at the next full moon. And maybe we'll bring the kumquat fudge."

"I'll be here, for sure, for sure," Carrie said, and they hopped on their bikes and everyone blew kisses at everyone else.

Phoebe and Grampa packed up the chairs and stuff, checked the campsite, and left everything the way they found it.

On the way back, Phoebe said, "We know some pretty good people, Grampa. And don't say what I already know you're thinking: 'Especially if they wear helmets.'"

"Well, yes, I might have said that. But tonight I would say, 'especially if they howl at the full moon, and could get a coyote excited.'"

"I'll bike to that," Phoebe said, and with lights brightening the bike path, they headed home.

ALBUM FIVE
GOOD DEEDS

At The Salvation Army

Cheap Grampa was sitting down working on the list of upcoming birthdays of his crew of grand kids. They were all getting too old for the usual one dollar beyond their ages. After all, one of them was just going to turn thirty. But Grampa wrestled with the idea of adding an extra dollar. Somehow thirty-two just sounded too cheap when you put the dollar sign before it, even for him.

But a man has to draw the line somewhere. And he suddenly felt sad thinking about how cheap he had been down that line. Like the year he made every kid a fan out of a piece of cardboard stapled to a tongue depressor. Of course he drew pictures on them with a magic marker, but really, a cardboard fan out of a tongue depressor, even if it really helped on a hot summer afternoon.

One of the kids had sent a snide 'thank you,' actually the only 'thank you' Cheap Grampa got that year. "Thanks for the fan, Gramps. I'm planning to bring mine on the trip the family is taking to Alaska. Thought I might sell it to an Eskimo. When I mentioned it to some of my brothers, they said I shouldn't. It would just depress the Eskimos." Gramps got the joke.

So next year he made a bunch of kites out of tissue paper he saved from last year's Christmas presents, and some string and some bamboo strips. He tied old neckties he bought at the Salvation Army as tails for the kites. String came from a butcher friend who went out of business. Grampa wrapped the kite string around empty toilet paper cores and the presents got a mild rise of thanks out of the kids.

One wrote, "Thank God, Gramps, we live in Chicago. Kites are big in the Windy City, and now I have one, thanks to you."

It was just the week he finished looking at the list when one of his granddaughters showed up with her mom. And fortunately, they had arrived on a Tuesday, and Gramps promised to take her and her mom to the Salvation Army store's "Half-off day" that happened every Wednesday. The kid was excited. She knew it would be good, but she didn't know it would be that good.

And Cheap Grampa was in a rare mood. He said words he had never said, "Honey, you just go buy anything you want. If it fits, buy it. Of course, not if it has a white tag. No white tags. You see, the Salvation Army uses tags that are color-coded. Each week, they pick four different colored tags to be on half sale. This week anything pink, blue, green or yellow tagged will be half off. But white tags will be full price."

She said, "You mean even if it's a fur coat, Grampa?"

"No, that you cannot buy, because the Salvation Army does not have fur coats and if it did you never would buy it because I know how much you love every living animal."

They all laughed and away the three of them went. It wasn't long before they were both shoving stuff into the shopping cart Grampa had brought up to where she was carrying two armfuls of bargain jeans, blouses and even a dress. And it was that dress that almost caused Grampa to lose his reputation, since, unfortunately, the dress she loved was a white tagged item. Cheap Grampa wrestled with his principles.

"You get it anyway, honey," he said with sorrow in his voice.

"Really Grampa? But it's full price."

"Listen, we saved so much money on everything else in your cart, we can afford to get that gorgeous dress at full price. Now, full price is all of $9.99, so it's still a bargain for a garment of that quality. Worth at least five of the drab things hanging next to each other at the Mall, selling for ten times this price, darling. So, if it fits, it's yours."

" Oh, Gramps, you're so generous."

"Shh. People will hear you. I'll be ruined. So shut up now, or I'll have to wash your mouth out with soap and water. And the soap won't even be biodegradable. I'm convinced. You deserve such a lovely dress, angel."

"Oh, Gramps, thanks, thanks, I so love it."

And she did love everything she bought, and it all fit, and she got a pair of half price shoes that would have broken the full allowance of every one of those rich college kids who go to college around here.

When it was all said and done, Grampa had to go find a trailer to rent to take it all home. But he bartered with The Trailer Guys and traded two hours use of the trailer for a great three-piece seersucker suit he himself had bought at the Salvation Army, even though he knew he would never wear it, but it was sooo cheap.

That's the way it goes with a Cheap Grampa, and a glorious granddaughter who believes that old adage: "Love Is the Wild Wind the Heart Rides Home on."

Camp

Cheap Grampa's granddaughter, one of them who lives in Ithaca, took Grampa to a new ice cream place. It was one of the things they did when he came to visit. This new place, she promised, actually had the flavor, kumquat fudge, which Lark knew was his favorite. "I don't quite know why it's your favorite, Grampa, but I honor your choices."

"It's a poifect choice. Fruit and chocolate in one place. Very money saving. A good example that life can really be two times the adventure and one third the cost."

She laughed, "I'm sorry this place is not going to be one third the cost. Maybe more like three times the cost."

"What, what, you mean they don't have any half gallons, buy one get one free?"

"Grampa, at this place, they don't even sell half gallons. To buy one would make people have to go take out a loan, or something."

Grampa looked shocked. "And this is where you're taking me. A poor victim of being born in the middle of the Great Depression, and I got to buy you ice cream at the king's confectionary?"

Suddenly, Lark got tender. "I'm paying Grampa."

"Oh, sweetie. That's so kind."

"Some of the kindness is because I need to con you about something. I want to be up front. For today's kumquat fudge ice cream, all you have to do is help me get to the summer camp I want to go to. It would mean so much to me, Grampa."

"Yeah, how much is so much. Enough to promise you'll

always wear your helmet at camp?"

"Gwan, you're kidding, aren't you?"

"No, I mean always. You have to wear it at dinner, in the shower, even when you're swimming."

"Oh, Gramps, you need an ice cream fix. Quit being silly. This is a camp where they do an overnight bicycle journey, and you know I'd wear it all through that."

Grampa patted her on the shoulder. "Good kid. I was kidding. Now how much money do you need?"

"Well, my family, because they know the director, even helped one of his kids once with some serious drug counseling, has been offered a half price scholarship. They have to come up with six hundred bucks more."

"Swell, count me in for one hundred dollars."

"That's generous, I know, Gramps, but it won't be enough. They're strapped. Four kids ain't no ride on no pink duck." She laughed, automatically making yet another old family joke. "Say, Grampa, did you ever go to camp when you were little?"

"I was never little. Those were dark and dreary times. Camp meant Dachau and Auschwitz, when I was growing up. I chose not to go."

She leaned over and gave him a sweet wet kiss. "I'm sorry you had that in your past, Grampa."

"Thanks, honey. You're a tender one. But, hey, I just remembered. I did go to camp one summer. It was a boy scout camp up in the Allegheny Mountains. And it was called Camp Twin Echoes. Do you want to hear the camp song?"

"Maybe you could hum a few bars, Gramps. We don't want to

empty the joint. But, I'm dying to know, where did you get the money to go, what with the horrible Great Depression and all?" Lark asked.

"Not from my grandfather, that's for sure. It's a long story, and after ice cream, I'll tell you."

And he did, after the kumquat fudge Lark paid for, and after Cheap Grampa asked to see the manager to congratulate him on being such a pioneer in ice cream flavors. "It's about time," Grampa said, when he shook the manager's hand.

"Oh, Lark. You bring back the memories. You're a great antidote to dementia. I remembered I got a scholarship, too. It was a Catholic camp. And I was not a Catholic, as you may have noticed. But, my best friend, Alfie, had a mother who knew how our family struggled. She told my mother that Alfie wouldn't go if I didn't go. And because she so wanted Alfie to be a big boy scout some day, 'I need your son to go, and I'll get him a scholarship.' And my mother gave in. She didn't know it was Catholic."

Lark laughed. "Sounds like Alfie's mom just might have conned your mother."

"As easily as you conned me. Lark, my darling, I will come up with the six hundred bucks. I just might have to do a little yard sale to pay for it, and you can help me tag the stuff, most of which I've collected from the dump. Is that a deal?"

She reached out and shook his hands. "It's a deal. And now, let me see if you remember how to cross yourself like you must have had to do in that camp when you pretended you were a Catholic."

And Grampa did. He showed her how he did it, way back then. "To you, your sister, and your brother, and kumquat fudge, Amen."

Band

One of the grand kids was in his Junior High School Band. He loved to show off for Cheap Grampa, playing his saxophone for him every chance he could. And that was, of course, because Grampa made such a big production out of every note.

"Oh, great, what a horn blower you are. Every jazz man in town would be jealous hearing you blow those notes, kid. Stan Getz would hang up his horn in envy. Benny Goodman would take his tenor sax to the pawn shop in utter despair."

"Grampa, Benny Goodman played the clarinet, not the saxophone."

"Clarinet schmarinet, you'd blow the reed out of any mouth piece. Damn, you're good, kid."

"You mean I'm damn good, Gramps."

"Don't let your parents catch you swearing, just keep playing them sweet notes."

"Well, Grampa, that's what I wanted to talk to you about."

"What, sweet notes? Now, if this is all leading up to something having to do with money, I don't want to hear about it."

The kid did a sweet riff on "Taking the A Train." And finished with a few wild notes from the overture from "The Music Man."

"It's just this, Grampa. The school says I've been using their saxophone for two extra semesters and it's time for me to get my own."

"What kind of school counts semesters for a genius like you? What if they had said that to Thelonius Monk?"

"Gramps, I don't think he ever used a school saxophone, and anyhow, I think the school's right. It's time. And the best thing of all, there's another kid in the band who just doesn't have the lips, Gramps, but he sure does have a very, very sweet horn."

Gramps interrupted, finishing his sentence. "And he wants to sell it to you very, very cheap, am I right?"

"Gramps, how did you ever guess?"

"Yeah, yeah," Cheap Grampa said, "but how cheap?"

"So cheap it wouldn't even take that bulge out of your wallet, Grampa."

"So, how cheap is that?"

"So cheap, you wouldn't even believe it comes with a case."

"Looking better, but come on, how cheap is that?"

"So cheap it comes with the two mouth pieces and three boxes of reeds."

"Now you're beginning to make some sense. But we have to do a little bargaining. Could he be convinced to swap you that very old and imperfect student model saxophone for a very nice German racing ten speed bike I just happened to have acquired?"

"No, Gramps, he's not very athletic. He wouldn't be interested in a ten-speed bike. Even one that won the Tour de France, which I know that one probably didn't."

"Ok, I get it, but how about a size thirty-nine three piece guaranteed seersucker suit, perfect for summer evenings and ball room dancing up at the lakeside dance hall."

"He doesn't dance. No, Gramps, he only wants money."

"Money, he wants?"

"Yes, Gramps, money. But cheap money of course."

"It's not even a question, but just how much do *you* have in order to buy this gem of a saxophone you are so hungry to own?"

"That's just it, Gramps, I don't have a cent."

"What, you spent all your bar mitzvah money already?"

"Gramps, you know I was never bar mitzvahed. My dad, your son, like you, doesn't believe in that stuff."

"So, your First Communion money? How about that?"

"You know my mom, your favorite daughter-in-law, who was never a Catholic, doesn't believe in that stuff either. So there's no money coming in from either source."

"How about the source of you working? Get a saxophone money-making job."

"I'm too young for that, Gramps. You have to be sixteen to get any kind of real job."

"You could work in the coal mines. They don't care if you lie about your age in West Virginia."

"Please, Gramps, get serious. We got a problem here. That really great saxophone is only a hundred bucks. And please, Grampa, don't start telling me how you sewed buttons on coats in the cellar of your tenement just to eat. I respect that, but it ain't going to help us get a saxophone."

Gramps looked at him, reached out and rubbed his crew cut head. "Who said we ain't going to get a hundred dollar saxophone. Would he take fifty bucks if we paid him cash, no check, no credit card, cash?"

"No, Gramps, he expects cash, and the price is a hundred bucks. Hey, I saved my parents money on this really close crew-cut hair-ruining job that will last all summer."

"That's good, horn man, but, how about the kid getting seventy-five bucks and a bike and a three piece seersucker suit thrown in?"

"No, gramps, a hundred genuine green backs. That's it. But don't forget the case, and the reeds that come with it."

"Well, I'll have to think about it."

"Oh, Gramps. Please think about it fast. Some other kid's going to have parents who are going to buy it for him. I know."

"What, someone who can't blow 'In the Mood' is going to get it? Someone who hasn't memorized the theme to 'The Phantom of the Opera'? OK, the answer is, yes, I'll take out a loan on my house and come up with the hundred bucks, but you have to agree to do something for me."

"Gramps, wait a minute, you have to take out a loan, a loan on your house, to come up with the money? I can't have you do that."

"Hey, I'm just pulling your spit valve. I got the hundred-dollar bill right here in the bulge in my wallet, like you said. But you do have to agree to something I need."

"Oh, boy, thanks, Gramps. I'll call the kid immediately. Ok, ok, but first, just tell me what it is you need."

"I like that you worry about me, too, just like I worry about you.

Well what I need is for you to learn John Denver's 'Annie's Song.'"

"Sure, Gramps, sure. I know I can learn it. If you can hum it, I can learn it. But, how come? I hear it's something they play at weddings. What do you need me to learn how to play 'Annie's Song' for?"

"It's for my wedding. We both love that song."

"Gramps. Gramps. You're getting married? You found someone willing to go along with your cheap ways?"

"What, what? You make it sound like a miracle has happened. Of course I found someone. We have a lot in common. She's one of the check-out persons at 'Deals and Steals, The Liquidation Center of All Liquidations.'"

He takes out his wallet. "Just kidding. Hey, will five twenty-dollar bills buy the miracle horn? If so, here they are. Can't wait to hear the first tune you'll blow just for your formerly cheap Grampa."

Off To Do A Mitzvah

We had been out on our bikes again. Phoebe so focused, watching out for the little furry caterpillars on the bike path. She would jam on her brakes and make us stop. She'd hop off and gently move them off into the bushes.

When we got to the end of the bike path we headed up a piece of highway. It was a new road for her, and she asked, "Where are we headed, Grampa?

"We're looking for the sign that points to the hospital, honey."

Suddenly, sounding anxious, she said, "What, are you sick or something Grampa?"

"Nah, I'm fit as a fiddle. Did you bring your fiddle, we could do a duet. Keep looking for that blue sign, please."

"I don't see it, Grampa. The sign has a big 'H' doesn't it?"

"What, you're going to get into a spelling bee? Yeah, a big H, with an arrow. It tells people where to turn when they're in an emergency. Do you see it yet?"

Cars were whipping by them. She said, "Isn't this a little dangerous, Grampa?"

"Life is dangerous. So? Keep your eyes peeled."

"I'd like to get back on the bike path."

"We can't."

"Why can't we?"

"I have two Mitzvahs to perform."

"Grampa, we don't have time for you get Bar Mitzvahed this afternoon"

"You don't even know what the word means, do you? Where have I failed? I've taught you to be cheap, but I never taught you about Mitzvahs?"

"I know what a Bar Mitzvah is. But, for a plain Mitzvah? Does it mean we got to go to a bar? You know I'm underage."

"Ha, ha, very funny. Now, shut up, quit complaining and keep looking for the H sign."

"Oh, there it is. I think that's it, but there are all these vines and bushes in front of it. No one could ever see it."

"And especially, someone in an emergency, all anxious, driving crazy, with someone bleeding in the back seat. That driver needs to be able to see the sign. We'll stop, now."

"Right here in all this traffic, Gramps?"

"That's where the sign is, my darling. Here, you keep an eye on our bikes."

And out of his back pocket he pulled a hedge clipper and he went to work on those vines and bushes. And in no time flat, there was the sign. With it's arrow pointing to the left. Just the way it should have been. Now it could be seen.

"That, my dearest granddaughter, that was a Mitzvah. And we don't tell people we did it. We just do it. Now, we have another one. You know my motto, 'buy one, get one free.'"

"Yes, Gramps, I know, I know, but where?"

"Follow me. We have to cross the road, and it's right over in that housing project. I planned to get them both done today, and I needed your help."

So, they got back on their bikes, waited for a break in the cars, and zoomed across. She said, rather tentatively. "Gramps, I heard it was dangerous to go into this project."

"All projects are not alike. We're safe here. They know me."

He wove in and out of several streets and she followed, looking out for wildlife on the road. They pulled up to one apartment building in the project. "This is it, girl."

Grampa reached into the basket behind his seat and pulled out a large red jug.

"What's that Gramps?"

"Some laundry detergent from my secret supply. There's a hard working single mom in here who has three kids and they all have only two sets of clothes. You know kids. They get dirty, and she wants to be able to send them off to school all bright and shiny. This jug will help her. It takes a lot each week."

They climbed the steps together, up to the third floor and rang a doorbell. A little kid answered from behind the door. "Who's there?"

"Hi, Jordy, it's Cheap Grampa. I got some laundry detergent for your mom and you kids. Open up."

The kid did and said, "Hi, Cheap, what's up?"

"Give this to your mom when she gets home for lunch. This is my granddaughter, Phoebe. Tell your mom Phoebe helped bring it over."

"Hi, Jordy," Phoebe said. "What's that you got in your hand?"

"It's a bird nest. It fell out of the tree. And this little bird was in it. It was crying. I picked it up. And I put it back in the nest.

I think I helped it. We got a lot of cats around here."

Phoebe said, very softly. "You did a Mitzvah, Jordy. And that's a good thing. I just learned about them. I already know a lot about birds. I'm pretty sure yours is a baby robin."

Jordy looked into the nest. "Really? A robin? I got a baby robin?"

Grampa said, "She knows birds, Jordy. She could help you and the birdie."

"Do you want to know how to feed little baby birds? I could teach you."

Jordy looked so happy. They spent a half hour there. The boy took her to his next-door neighbor and Phoebe told her what a Mitzvah Jordy had done for the baby robin. Then they borrowed a can of cat food. As luck would have it, there was a kid down the hall who was just finishing a popsicle. Phoebe convinced him to give her the popsicle stick, and with that and the cat food, she showed Jordy how to feed his first bird.

"You're a natural, Jordy. Maybe you'll become a Wild Life Re-Habber or a Veterinarian some day. Here's my phone number, call me if you need more help." She wrote her number down on one of the used three by five cards Cheap Grampa always had in his back pocket.

"Thanks, Mitzvah girl. Please come back. You're real cool." He gave her five.

And on the bike path to home, Grampa said, "Baby, you were great. I see you are destined to get into the Mitzvah hall of fame."

"I don't think there is one. Not if Mitzvahs are things you do without people knowing. Oh well, but what fun, and Gramps, we got a total of three for the day. Not too shabby. Almost makes me feel Jewish."

"Almost?"

"Well, time will tell," she said.

Back on the bike path, Cheap Grampa reminded her, "It was really four, honey. Remember the fuzzy caterpillar. They sure are sweet, all Mitzvahs are, right up there with the buy one get one free at the Super Market."

Cheap Grampa and the Call Center Miracle

Grampa was not hopeful as he dialed the 1-800 number. Call Centers have not been, what could he say, they have not been exactly centered.

"Good afternoon, welcome to Customer Service, my name is Emmalina. We're committed to customer satisfaction here."

He couldn't resist saying, "You're kidding, aren't you? You're not serious, right?"

"Sir, I believe in customer satisfaction. How can I help you? But, first, what are the last four of your Social?"

"But, what if I'm not feeling very social today."

"Well, we'll change that, sir. What's the problem? Forget about your social security number."

"I almost have," he said, and then decided not to waste any time. "I think I've been grossly overcharged."

Emmalina said, her voice syrupy, "Oh, I'm so happy. That's one of my specialties. You are in luck. I have your bill right in front of me. And I see it's almost double from last month's"

He said, "Oh, Emmalina, you noticed. This is going to be good, I can feel it."

"Now let's see. Oops, $39.80 for those nineteen information calls."

"Yes, yes," he moaned. "They must have been made by my daughter. If I've told her once I..." And then before he could finish his sentence, Emmalina's first miracle glowed.

"Well, I'll just deduct that charge. Don't punish her, sir, I was an air-head once."

"You were?" Grampa asked, astonished. "And now you're so understanding. But so is my beloved spendthrift daughter. Emmalina, I promise I won't even yell at her."

She said, "That would be wise, sir. Trust me. You don't want her running away."

He waited a moment, then said, "Oh, Emmalina, you didn't did you?"

"Yes, I did, sir, twice."

"And that's how you got trapped in Customer Service, Emmalina?"

"Don't feel sorry for me, Gramps. Customer service has been my salvation. Every time I deduct some pain, my self-esteem increases."

"Well, Emmalina, can I increase your self-esteem even more?"

"Oh, yes, yes," she said. "Where? Show me."

"Well, on page six. The activation fee for the new phone. It's for my son-in-law, and the agent I spoke with said he would waive the fee."

She interrupted, "Yes, I see it, right on page six. I can fix that."

He said, "You can?"

"I will. Let me refresh my screen, wait, don't hang up."

He mumbled, "I may never hang up."

"There it's done, and I feel so much better. Your bill is now down almost $65."

"Wonderful news, Emmalina. I'll pay it before it all slips away."

"Usually there's a $5 fee for agent-assisted bill paying, but I can waive that, too."

She didn't even ask, "credit or debit?"

When that was done, Cheap Grampa said to her, "I have to speak to your supervisor, Emmalina. I have to tell him or her that I met a miracle this afternoon. You gave the most brilliant customer service I have ever known. I want to tell that supervisor that they've trained you right. I am so customer satisfied."

There was a long silence. Neither one of them wanted to hang up. Grampa didn't want to be selfish. But, then she spoke.

"I'm a little embarrassed, sir. You see, I *am* the supervisor. We were short handed today, and I was just helping out."

"G'wan," he said. "You're kidding me. You're not serious?"

"Ok," she said, shyly. "I *was* teasing you. But you don't have to tell my supervisor. I'm engaged to marry him, so he already knows how good I am."

And she laughed, and Grampa laughed, and then he said, "Thanks, Emmalina. Thanks for being who you are. And today for this Cheap Grampa, you've been a miracle. You've restored my faith in Call Centers."

Religion at Starbucks

Someone started to talk religion while Cheap Grampa was sitting in Starbucks drinking his coffee out of the jug he brought from home. The management had long ago given up trying to talk Cheap Grampa out of this outlandish habit, but he had slowly convinced them that if this town had a Senior Center he would go there. But it doesn't and he can't see how he would ever be a bad influence on their regular customers. "A little bit of uniqueness is what I bring to any joint. They see me as local color and even tell their friends to come to this Starbucks for the entertainment."

So he drinks from his Mason jar and butts into any conversation he wants to. Fortunately, not too many Tea Party aficionados come to this Starbucks, so his brilliant comments defending Obama, setting people straight on Haliburton seals on oil rigs in the Gulf of Mexico, etc. are generally tolerated.

But this morning, someone was talking about religion. His ears not what they once were, picked up just a phrase from the conversation, and since one of the speakers he recognized as the minister from the Episcopalian church, who usually spoke stuffed shirt stuff from above his white collar, Cheap Grampa decided to take his Mason jar of coffee over to their table, and said, "Good morning, gentlemen. May I join you?" Without waiting for an answer, he sat and went right to it.

"I overheard that one of you said something about something descending from the clouds and I wondered if you'd mind if I put my one cent in. I'm cheap and I don't spend two cents on anything until I know it's on sale."

The minister put out his hand, "Baker is my name."

"I know you, Father, you run that thing with the steeple up the street, right?"

"Well, no, actually the steeple belongs to my friend, Rev. Loman." He pointed to the other guy. "That's his steeple."

"People call me Cheap Grampa. Nice to meet you both."

Rev. Loman said, "And you're right, we *were* talking about stuff that was descending from clouds, but it wasn't so much religion."

"No," Father Baker said, "we were talking about the rain that came down and the damage it did to some of the people we know. One of my parishioners owns the car salvage place just south of Greenfield, and the river overflowed the banks right in that area and all kinds of cars and car parts were floating right across Route 5. It's a disaster up there."

Rev. Loman came right in. "And one of my farmers lost over 100 acres of corn he had planted in one of his low lying fields."

Baker interrupted, "One of my farmers had 400 acres of potatoes drowned."

They both waited for Cheap Grampa to say something. And what he had to say got the three of them talking all afternoon. Because he said, "And you don't think that's religion?"

Once he got them arguing about what scripture said about floods and parting of waters, etc., Cheap Grampa excused himself and went over to another table where two young couples were talking about how one couple there had almost drowned when they were the first car to come to a place up in Vermont where the road had completely washed out. They had spent three hours in the rain, warning other cars on both sides of the washout, one on the north and one on the south, waving flashlights, until the State Police arrived and posted yellow tape from tree to tree a whole mile up the road on both sides, barely thanking the kids, "But, hell, they had their hands full, that night."

Cheap Grampa said, "Your table is really talking about religion in action. I congratulate you. Say, I bet you could use some new batteries for your flashlight, and I just got some at the flea market. Being from the flea market they might not really work, but, here they are, and they were damn cheap. You two, with your big hearts, must have descended from the clouds."

The woman looked at Cheap Grampa, and reached for his hand. "You seem to have some clouds stuck to you, too, Gramps."

"Happens every day if you sit at the right table. Thanks, you two." His coffee was done. He had another place to get to. He waved to everyone, and at the door looked up to see what the clouds were doing.

ALBUM SIX
LIFE LESSONS

County Fair

It won't be long now before the county fair comes to that town up the road about twenty miles from us. I'm starting to see the early publicity. There was a picture in the newspaper of a kid joyously riding on the merry-go-round with cows all around staring at him. I cut it out and sent it off to the granddaughter who most digs that kind of fair. She loves the animals. I've committed to taking her and one of her local friends.

My own kids, years ago, spent their money at "Joey Chitwood and the Demolition Derby" kind of fairs. Times change, but some of my cheap practices do not. I will require the granddaughter and her friend to each carry her money around her neck in an old 35mm. film can that Kodak used to put Kodachrome in. I drill a hole in the lids, and hang them from an old shoestring.

Now, Rule #1. Before they can spend a single penny, they have to walk around the entire fair grounds. Just think of the logic of that. With that genius rule there's no impulse buying, no being sucked into the smell of fried dough before you see what else you might want to eat. No scary rides, yet. The walk around is fun. Each kid gets to figure out what she really, really, *really* wants to spend her money on. And her time on.

Rule #2. About the money. Each kid gets the same amount of money to start with, and no more. So, once you blow the bucks, you could beg until dawn, and Cheap Grampa would not come up with another penny. Rules are rules. Budget, balance, and be wise.

Rule #3. The games of chance are to be recognized as rip-offs. Your possibility of winning the giant stuffed Panda is about 600 to 1. Maybe even 650 to 1.

My granddaughter is as wise as they come. Also, determined.

Last year she became really determined to beat one of the games of chance. It was a polished stainless steel spiral rod game. You were given a magnetized wand in your hand and a small cylinder was dropped from the top of the spiral. Your job was to use the wand to keep the ring as it wound its way down the spiral from touching the center.

The guy running the booth could bring it down time after time without touching the spiral. And he agreed to let her practice twice before she had to put up her money. Gently, I took her aside and said, "Granddaughter of my heart. You will not win, you will lose your money, money you will not have for all the other things around this fair."

Determined young woman she is, she said, "Grampa, I know you're cheap, but I know I can win. I know I can do it. And I want that giant stuffed Panda."

"My darling granddaughter," I said. " One compromise. Go play with the rabbits, goats and sheep, and in one hour, come back, I will be here with you, rooting you on." She agreed. And off she and her friend went.

An hour later, with straw in her hair, she said, "I'm ready, Gramps." She practiced a little, then put her five dollars for two tries down and with determination in her eye, she did her two tries and almost won, but she didn't get the Panda.

On the ride home, we all talked about it. "Gramps, for the rest of my life I might have thought that I could have won that Panda. Well, I didn't, but I tried."

I pulled into a Creemie joint, and bought one Creemie, on me, for all of us to share. For each lick, we had to recall a sweet memory of our day together. That's one sweet way to celebrate a special day. I heartily recommend it as a way to seal in the sweetness of any perfect day, and, of course, it's a cheap way, oh yes.

Vocabulary Drill

Lark and Grampa were off on one of their 'testing out a new part of the bike trail' rides. "This looks interesting, Gramps. Where are we headed to? I like the leafy canopy overhead."

Grampa said, "Makes me sad. Down in Florida a lot of trees were taken out by Hurricane Charley. We lost the lovely cathedral-like quality the bike path had down there. But, it reminds me, I've wanted to play Vocabulary with you. Are you up for it this morning?"

"Oh, Grampa, you're trouble, but I love you so much, I'll play. We'll take turns, of course."

"Of course. You can even have two turns to my every one."

Lark answered, "That wouldn't be right, Grampa."

"So you always try to be right? Is that what you're saying?"

She said, "Well, maybe to be totally accurate, I don't like to be wrong."

"Ok, now vocabulary has started. What's the opposite of wrong"

She said, "Well, the easy answer is 'right.' Right?"

"And the harder answer? Notice, hard is the opposite of easy?"

"So this vocabulary drill is about opposites? That could be fun, Grampa."

"Keep pedaling. It could get complex."

She said, "So, is simple a good opposite of complex?"

"Watch that root sticking up in the path. Avoidance may not

be simple."

"Hey," she said, "Smooth is the opposite of bumpy on a bike trail."

Grampa asked, "And the opposite of disaster is?"

She gave her famous tolerance look, sighed and said, "Always wearing your bike helmet and keeping your eyes peeled." She laughed then, "No one said the opposite has to be just one word."

"Point well taken, as always."

She said, "And one opposite of 'always' could be 'occasionally?'"

"I like it, I like it," Grampa said, "and the opposite of 'point well taken' is: 'Shut up.' But I would never say that to you, my darling granddaughter."

"Thanks, Grampa. I might never say that to you, as well. Because the opposite of someone who says 'Never' could be, 'They're lying.'"

"Now, there's a point very, very, *very* well taken." Grampa said. "My mentor, way back in graduate school, taught us about unqualified words like: 'never, always, completely, absolutely, and positively.' He used to say, and it makes me smile thinking about it, 'Before a judge you should raise your right hand and say, 'I promise to tell the near truth, the approximate truth, and nothing but the relative truth, so help me future experience.'"

Lark stopped to rescue one of her furry caterpillars and gently put it off in the grass alongside the path. Grampa noticed, and said, "You done right, girl."

"Thanks," and then, she said, "That mentor of yours was one smart man. I remember his name, because you've told me other stories about him and his impact on you, Louis Raths."

"Thanks, honey. Raths needs to be remembered. He was so way ahead of his time. He knew so much about what was right and wrong. But he rarely preached. He kept inventing strategies and tools to help kids figure out what was really right and really wrong for themselves."

"Keep pedaling, Gramps, because I know we're not done getting to where we're going to, and Vocab game isn't done yet, but please tell me one of his strategies or tools."

"Funny you should ask. I was just getting ready to. Imagine this," he said, "there's Professor Raths in one of those college lecture rooms, a hundred students waiting for his next words, and Raths says, 'Take out a piece of paper and draw a line down the middle.'"

"Gramps, should we stop and do it right now?"

"Nah, the opposite of right now is, 'A little later, when we get home.'"

"Ok, I got it. I'm listening."

Grampa said, "With most people I would say, 'they almost listen.' But with you, I could unqualifiedly say, 'you always listen.'"

"Woids, woids," she said. "Tell me what we write on the paper for Raths' strategy."

"And the opposite of 'impatience' is?" he asked.

"Patience is a necessary expeeeeerience," she said, sounding just like the robotic voice from a long ago World's Fair exhibit her grandma had taught Lark to say.

"I get it, I got it. Ok, back to work. Now, on the left hand side of the paper, you make a list. A marvelous list, of the initials of everyone who has had a meal at your table in the last year. Now, it could be a long list or a short list. It can include lunches you gave to friends of your friends, etc. Can you imagine it?"

"Yepper, I can. Now, what's on the other side?"

"Well, first, he had us code the names on the left side. I remember it well, almost sixty years ago. You put 'F' for family, 'FR' for friends, 'C' for colleagues, 'A' for acquaintances. 'O' for others. Get it?"

"Got it. I can see the list at our house," Lark said. "A lot of people who love birds and justice."

"Hmm. Then, the other column. Most interesting. 'List the initials of homes where you have eaten a meal.' Now, of course, there is a similarity, a reciprocity.

"But still, often, one list is longer, and that opens up some issues. But then, Raths threw us the curve ball. As he often did. And it was right up our Vocabulary Game alley. He asked people to write down their definitions and to explain the difference between *desegregation* and *integration*."

"Wow, Gramps. I feel the power. And all of this in the face of those initials of the people who eat at your house. We're not prejudiced, but we're not integrated either."

"Do you see why I love you? And around the next corner we'll be at the place I wanted us to see today."

They came to the curve in the path, near the river, and where a big bridge crossed over it, above their heads. And down in the valley, a cluster of not very new cars, and a couple of clotheslines with clothes blowing in the wind.

"What is that, Grampa, a campground down there?"

"Not exactly."

"It looks like people are down there. Do they live there?"

"Not exactly."

"Don't get cute with me. What's going on?"

"You ready for this? Maybe we should begin making two lists on a sheet of paper. 'What's Right in our Society', and 'What's Wrong in our Society.'"

Lark said, "My instincts say, what's going on down there is wrong."

Grampa said, "Very wrong. Those cars are homeless people living and sleeping in their cars. Clustered together for some safety, and never knowing when they will be kicked out."

"Oh, Grampa, that's really, really wrong."

"And we have to think of something, as small as it is, to make it a little bit righter. Do we go down and talk to someone down there to see what we could do to help?"

"How big a difference could one granddaughter and one Cheap Grampa make?" she asked.

"The concept of 'Nothing' has it's opposite in the word 'Something.' Let's go, kid, and we'll see."

About the Shade

Grampa had put the bike rack on his old Toyota convertible, and he was hanging the last of the two brightly painted red bikes he fixed up, when his granddaughter, the thirteen-year-old, came out and said, "Here are the two bungees you asked for, Gramps. That sure is some fire engine paint you used on those two bikes. They're both girls' bikes. Which one am I going to ride today?"

"You'll get the one with the two good tires. And lucky me, I'll ride the ones with the flat tires."

"You're kidding, of course?"

"Of course, what else do I have you around for? I kid. And I love you."

"I love you right back, you old biker, you. So where are we going?"

He answered, with a look in his eyes, "To uncharted territory. And let's get moving. You, please, go and get the helmets. Ours and three extra ones in case we need a couple."

"Ok, I won't ask any questions, I'll just let the mystery grow. But why do we need extra helmets? Oh, I know the answer already, 'You'll see.' It's always that, or, 'we'll see.'"

But, cheerful as always, she brought the helmets and helped him with the last bungees, and then said, "I packed us a lunch, as requested, boss."

"The usual?"

"Yep, the usual. Provolone wrapped around smoked salmon and graced with apricots and pecans. And enough to even give a couple away, if we need to. Plus, an apple and an orange for each of us. Water, too. We're all set. I'm ready, are you?"

"You're good. So, consequently, I'll let you hold the map. And maybe, you'll find out where we're going as we get closer to it." He hopped in, put his seat belt on before he started the engine. Glanced over at her, and she was already wearing hers. The engine started, gurgled and burped a little as he backed it out of the driveway and onto the road. They were quiet together for a while, until they got to the bridge. There were lots of boats out and people fishing from the causeway. Grampa said, "Today is about one cent a pound more."

She waited. He didn't say anything more. "Ok, I'll go with that. I don't know what it means, but I know, before the sunrises again, you'll tell me."

"Even sooner," he said. "But not yet." She had learned to be content with that.

She liked looking at everything that she could see out the windows, and she spotted every bird and living thing that was there, and named them. An anhiga, a big blue heron. An osprey, a turkey vulture. And she said, "I saw a sign for Rt. 29. And I found it on the map. We're going northeast. And some town, down this road, has the longest name I've seen in Florida yet, Gramps. It's called Immokalee. Did I pronounce it right?"

"Yeah, but they should have named it, 'Big Shame Little Hope.'"

"Why 'Big Shame and Little Hope', Gramps?"

"You'll see. Pretty soon."

"I see a lot of fields. And now, I see some people working in the fields. They're carrying big baskets on their shoulders. What's in them, Gramps?"

"I could answer that in a lot of ways. One cent more a pound, for starters. Modern day slavery, is another way. Human trafficking. Lousy immigration laws."

She said, "One at a time, Gramps. Now, I see it's tomatoes they're picking, and I gather when they fill a basket, they carry it to the big truck. And I bet if they got one cent more a pound it could make a difference, but one cent doesn't sound like much. Sounds more like the kind of weekly allowance you gave my mother and her brothers. Ho ho."

"Ok, wise guy, but this is real. One cent a pound more could almost double their pay at the end of the week. Isn't that amazing?"

"Well, why don't they give it to them? You and I would pay the extra penny when we buy our tomatoes, wouldn't we?"

"Of course we would. But the greed of the big corporate tomato users is fighting it. They've had some big breakthroughs after some long fights. Taco Belle and Macdonald's have agreed to only buy tomatoes from growers who pay the extra penny. But there are lots who won't. One of the worst is the local grocery chain, Publix. A lot of my friends are boycotting the store, but not enough people are. Habits are hard to change."

"Can we stop and just look for a while, Gramps? I got thirsty, just watching those guys picking in this heat."

"That's another thing the workers don't get. No place in the shade to take a break and get some water. I don't see the shelter tent so I don't think we'll be welcome here. Let's go beyond this field and we'll hop on the bikes and just do a little country ride to see what we can see."

"Great, I knew today was going to be an adventure."

A couple of miles down the road, they parked in some shade, got out, and unloaded the bikes, put their helmets on, and started off down the road. A few miles further down the road, they saw another field and a lot of pickers. The same baskets, the same big truck, but they noticed there was a shade tent.

They went in to talk to someone. They learned a lot. This was a recognized field where changes had happened, according to a guy they talked to. He was from the Redlands Christian Migrant Association. He told them about the seventy-four childcare centers they operated and how much they mattered to the pickers we all saw out in the field. Grampa and Phoebe could see some of the hope on the faces of the pickers, who waved at them, and smiled when they waved back.

It turned out it was just what Grampa was looking for. They agreed to come back with the two bikes and leave them with a man whom they met. He said there were lots of kids who'd love to have a chance to share the bikes. The idea was they could leave them outside the community house, and anyone could sort of rent them for a day, like at a library. Grampa told the man about the extra helmets they would leave, as well. "No helmet worn, no rental," Grampa said.

The man from the Association smiled. "I think we can do that. There have been harder things we've tackled."

"Just what the world needs," Grampa said. "A free bike rental place. And an honor system to get it back in exactly twenty-four hours."

Grampa and Phoebe shook hands all around. She gave the Migrant Association guy one of their Provolone Specials. He laughed and said, "Maybe we could add this to the menu at the soup kitchen we run."

They waved to everyone again and started back to the car, talking excitedly the whole time. "Gramps," she said, "I know what we did was just a drop in the bucket, but it's the right bucket."

"There's always more to get done," he said, "but we've started on our personal tomato journey. That's why I used that red paint on the bikes."

She said, "Leave it to you. And when we take on the forces of evil in the citrus business, I know what color the next bikes will be."

Validations Defined and In Action

Cheap Grampa was telling one of his buddies out at the town dump just how wonderful his granddaughter was. Stu Franklin didn't have any granddaughters. He did brag a lot about his boy grand kids, always winning some wrestling, fencing or gymnastic event.

Franklin was a big bragger, and Cheap Grampa a good listener, but after a while, he said, "Franklin. You got a big mouth. Now, get a big ear. It's my turn." Franklin started to open his mouth to complain, but Cheap Grampa made a fist and threatened to punch Franklin in the mouth. "Just shut up, Stu. You'll get another turn."

That's when Cheap Grampa pulled out the egg timer he had just found at the dump before Franklin got there. "Look, I think this timer might work for us."

Franklin said, "What, I have to wait until you make a hard boiled egg before I can talk?"

"No, just three minutes, Stu. And then you'll get three minutes. Fair is fair."

Stu wasn't totally convinced, but he quickly grabbed the timer and turned it over, checking to see that sand was flowing, and it was. "Wonder why someone would throw this out. Looks like it's working."

Cheap Grampa sounded irritated, as he often was with Franklin. "It's my three minutes and you're already doing all the talking. Start it over. I want my whole time. And shut up."

Franklin wasn't happy, but he did as he was told. "Ok, are you ready, motor mouth? One, two, three." He flipped the timer and said, "Tell me."

And Cheap Grampa did. "You've heard me tell you stories about my Phoebe, my thirteen-year-old granddaughter? Just nod, yes or no. No words, Stu." Stu nodded yes, and took out a cigar, lit it, blew a smoke ring and sat down on a stack of old tires.

Well, Cheap Grampa started, speaking rapidly, needing to get in as much as he could in his three minutes. "She just turned thirteen, and I made her a crown out of an old pie plate I found out here, spray painted it gold color, and jazzed it up with some colorful stones from my hobby collection. And I dubbed her, with a wooden spoon, as 'The Queen of Validation.' And, Franklin, no questions. If you don't know what validation is, look it up when you get home." Franklin just looked bored.

"Ok, Phoebe has just turned thirteen and that's hardly enough years to get that complicated concept nailed and daily delivered, but oh, my, has she got it down pat.

"When I phone her, she never fails to say, 'I'm so glad you called, Cheap Grampa.' Our usual banter goes: 'I'm so honored that you picked up the phone.' To which she quickly says, 'The honor is all mine.' That is quickly followed, as it was just the other day with, 'And thanks for the box you sent up with our friendly mailman. Certainly, you hit the bull's-eye with your brilliant inclusion of my favorite flavored Nips, but that very handy thing to back up my computer onto is fantastic. You are something else, Grampa, truly awesome.'"

Franklin pointed to the timer. "Talk fast, Bozo."

Cheap Grampa said, "Don't waste any of my time. I'm talking. I'm talking, and when Phoebe and I talk, a lot of it is about how the birds are doing, and she tells me about the new boarders the main bird woman of Vermont brought to her, all on a motorcycle because she and her husband were going off on a birthday trip. More baby birds, but also a whole bucketful of meal worms, absolutely essential for the twenty-six baby birds she already has, so they can learn how to eat bending down to feed. It's getting to be the time to say goodbye to the gawking wide-open mouths, the scraping of slush food off on the side of the beak from the half sized popsicle stick she uses. She gives me all the details. Linda brought her more syringes, band-aid stuff, and above all, the affirmation that she trusts our Phoebe like we all do. Phoebe rattles off the validations she holds for Linda, and then rushes in to thank me for my contribution to the new cage that will, and unless you were there, you wouldn't possibly understand (that's not a de-validation, it's just a description of reality) the cage that will become a place for the crow they've had who has had up til now the whole outside screened porch all to himself, but which is desperately needed by the emerging birds, grown big now, needing a space to try their wings, more and more, wings that need to recognize when a wall looms up so they don't knock themselves out while learning to fly."

Franklin was shaking the timer. "Now, I know why this was at the dump. The sand is stuck and it ain't running. When's my turn coming, Cheapo?"

"Look, Franklin. I'll give you twice the time you give me, like I always do anyhow. Let me finish. Or do I really have to knock your teeth out to make you shut up, and let me finish."

Franklin whacked the timer on one of the tires, and the sand started to flow again.

"I guess it was just trying to make a pearl in there," and he laughed at his own joke.

Cheap Grampa said, "Where was I?"

"She was buttering you up about how good she is with the birds, and I bet, pretty soon, it's going to cost you some money."

"So what? Ok, I remember, I was going to tell you how I thanked her for thanking me. 'You're so welcome Phoebe. I always feel so totally recognized with your incredibly wise inclusions.' That may be the very essence of true validation. The theory says it's different from praise. Much to our surprise, praise often has a hooker in it. 'How nice of you to put your underwear in the hamper, Johnny.' And implied is, 'And you better do it every darned time or else.' Validation, on the other hand has no hooker. It is simply the spontaneous delight in another human being, and taking the time to tell them so."

Franklin tapped out the ash on his cigar and blew two more perfect smoke rings.

"All right, so I don't have to look up the definition of validation. You told me. Will that be on the test?"

"You'd flunk the test if it was, Franklin. Let me finish. There's one more part, and then I'll sit here as you go through bragging about all your wrestlers, fencers, gymnasts and probably six swimmers and five football quarterbacks you have.

"But I'm talking about my world champion here, the Queen of Validation. On our run up to get supplies for the bird migration, (Okay, sometimes you have to spend money to have good results) she sprinkled me with her observations of me in action. Never missing one. 'You were so nice to that check out girl, Grampa. I could see how much she appreciated you. You're a funny kind of guy, you know?' The back story is the young girl had said 'No, we don't have any,' when we asked where the meal worms were. Fortunately, another male clerk had overheard the question, and he said, 'Oh, of course we have them.' Phoebe went off with the guy, but ever aware of anything good, overheard me say to the clerk, 'Hey, there's so much to learn. Whew, and I bet you've learned a lot here.' She smiled. 'Yes, I have.' Phoebe reminded me that I added to it, 'I've kept on learning all my life.'

"We had one more stop to make, because on our shopping list was a pair of scissors for her mom. At Staples, I pulled out the flyer, and there was a whole page of 50% off stuff, and lo-and-behold, they had titanium scissors on sale, 50% off. We bought two pairs.

"Bushels of validations came with that. 'What a shopper you are, Grampa. Thanks for teaching me to look for the 50% off signs. You may be cheap, but you're so smart at being cheap.' I ask you, Franklin. Whom would you nominate for the Queen of Validations?"

"Not you, Cheapo. Now can I talk? Here, take the timer, and I get three flips, right?"

"Four if you don't bore me to tears, Stu." One of the things I like about Franklin is, he doesn't even hear sarcasm.

"Thanks for the validation," he said, and started bragging.

The Traffic Cop

Cheap Grampa and his granddaughter had been to the theater. It was that play about the dog. Not Lassie. Not Sounder. It was A.R.Gurney's play, <u>Sylvia</u>.

This kid loves anything with fur. I can't say she loves anything with four legs, because as an assistant Wildlife Rehabber, she often has to take care of three legged creatures, wounded squirrels, damaged possums and little almost road-killed rabbits.

She had lots to say about the play, digging that an actress could play a dog, and do the kind of clever and sometimes deceitful things a smart dog can do. The play includes the dog having jealous feelings about the wife of the guy who brought Sylvia home. Cheap Grampa and she discussed the whole idea of believing that a dog can have serious human traits, feelings, and behaviors that go with deep feelings.

That's when the traffic cop pulled them over. Phoebe said, "Gramps, what did you do wrong? Why are those blue lights flashing?"

With a twinkle in his eye, he said. "Don't say anything about the illegal rum this bootlegger brought in from the mainland, honey bun."

"Gramps, this is no laughing matter, being stopped. I know that if you get a ticket, it won't be cheap. Your reputation is at stake. Oh, oh, here comes The Law."

"Good evening, officer, what can my granddaughter and I do for you tonight, sir?

The officer was taken aback by Grampa. Then Phoebe said, "He really means it, sir. My grampa helps people all the time."

"That's very nice, little girl. But he better start helping himself first. Sir, you were doing 40 in a 25 mph zone. The radar actually said 42, but 40 will do nicely for a ticket. License and registration, please."

Cheap Grampa reached in his fanny pack, unzipped it, and the officer said, "You don't have a gun in there, do you?"

Phoebe spoke up. "Oh, officer, my beloved grampa wouldn't even touch a gun. He's been a peacenik ever since he was in the Navy back in World War II."

Cheap Grampa said, "Phoebe, please let the officer do his duty." And he handed him his driver's license and the registration. The officer said, "Thanks, now wait right here."

Phoebe said, as the officer started walking back to the flashing lights, "It's a school night, sir. Could my grampa just get me home?"

"Young lady," he said, "This is serious business. There's something for you to learn here tonight."

"You mean, like seeing how quickly that 25 mph zone came up at us?"

Cheap Grampa nudged her. "Shh, my darling. We'll sit and wait." And they talked some about what a traffic cop's life must be like.

The officer handed back the registration and drivers' license, and asked, "When was the last time you got a ticket? I can't find anything on you."

Cheap Grampa laughed. "Oh, I remember it well. It was the year Al Gore ran against George the Bush."

The officer guffawed. "Ok, I bite. Tell me the story."

"I remember the time," Cheap Grampa said, "because I had a big 'Vote for Al Gore' bumper sticker." He turned to Phoebe. "I was visiting your Ithaca cousins, honey, and coming back, I was going through a small town that had this legendary speed trap. A sudden 25 mph sign within ten feet of a 40 mph sign. I knew about the trap, because I had gotten a ticket there four years earlier, and I know it was because I had a big 'Vote Bill Clinton' bumper sticker on the back of this very same car."

Phoebe said, "I love how you stand up for what you believe in, Grampa."

"And that includes that I'm cheap, too, right?"

"Right."

The officer said, "And you think you got those traffic tickets because you had the wrong bumper sticker?"

"No, officer, I had the right bumper sticker. The traffic cop just didn't believe it.

Phoebe said, "I helped him put on that new Obama sticker on the back of his car."

Grampa said, "We're both believers."

Phoebe said, "And letter writers. I just wrote the President an urgent letter, because he's making some really bad environmental decisions, like Tar Sands, and Monsanto and GMO's -- but don't get me started!"

The officer said, "That's very impressive, Ma'am. But it seems you just don't feel as strongly about speed limits."

Phoebe argued back. "Yes we do, sir. And we believe in seat belts, religiously, and bicycle helmets for all occasions."

"That's quite a granddaughter you got there, Gramps." He turned to look hard at Phoebe. "Well, I think a warning should do in this case tonight."

"I feel warned, Officer," Cheap Grampa said.

"Well, we'll see. A second offense after you've been warned is a big red flag in our computer."

Phoebe said, "I'll keep a double eye on him officer. I ride shotgun for him a lot, and I feel I should have gotten the ticket if you were going to give him one. I should have seen that sign that said 25 mph. It just caught me by surprise. I bet that even happened to the stage coach shotgun riders in the old West."

The officer reached out and shook Cheap Grampa's hand, and looked at Phoebe. "I'd keep this one, Gramps."

Phoebe said, warmly, "Thanks. He keeps telling me I'm a 'Chippie off the old block.'"

Cheap Grampa said, "I have to keep a double eye on her, too, Officer."

"Well, good night to both of you. And, if by chance you see the President, tell him he got my vote, too." He drove off.

"You saved the day, girl, with your brilliant input."

"No, silly goose, I just tried to keep you cheap."

ALBUM SEVEN
FAMILY PHONE CALLS

Not Really

The granddaughter was on the phone. "I'm sorry I've been out of touch, Gramps."

"Very busy up there? Birds and all?"

"Not really, we're down to twenty-two birds, and two new baby rabbits, but we did get a seriously wounded pigeon that came in yesterday, and we had to rush off to the vet's to get a bone set. Whew, what a journey that was."

"So, how is he?"

"We don't know if it's a he or a she, Grampa."

Grampa took a moment and then asked, "Does it matter?"

"No, not really. A bone to be set can cross genders."

"Ok, so twenty-two birds and how many furry things?"

"You mean, mammals?"

"Not really, there might be other furry things. I happen to know you got a chicken. Do you call your chicken furry?" he asked.

"Not really. Still a bird. And to answer your question, specifically, we call her 'Peep.' But, Gramps, that's not what I wanted to talk to you about."

"Really?"

"Yes, really. Now, no smart alec stuff, ok? Please listen. It's about coming to Florida."

"What, you changed your mind? Now I get my money back? I don't have to waste gas coming to the airport and raising more money to buy more gas to get you back when you have to break my heart by leaving? What, you changed your mind? After I arranged for you to be the guest speaker at the Trailer Park Parrot Show? What, now you take a great notion to cancel on me right on the eve of the incredible creativity party, to which I've invited the whole Island? And the only reason I'm scheduling a creativity party is because you're going to be there and I bought a new used piano with almost eighty-eight keys, just because you will play your piano and Mozart up my living room in what will be the high point of the whole creativity night, even with the competition of the finest poets, short story writers, jugglers, guitar players and famous oil painters present on our Island. What, you'd cancel your visit just to shame me in their presence and deny them your famous coconut balls as dessert for forty people, coming out of the woodwork, just to meet my famous granddaughter?"

A long and very deep sigh filled the telephone wires. Finally, a voice from the North. "Grampa, please, I don't want to say, 'shut up', but if you don't stop I may have to do it, and not real gently, either, and if you don't quit jabbering, then I'll pull the phone plug."

"What, your family, my life support system, and you'd pull the plug, if I don't shut up? After all I've done to you, this is the gratitude I am shown?"

"All right, I've heard that speech before. And I'm sorry, I don't like to use negative criticism, but Gramps I've had to correct you too often. It isn't 'done to you.' Silly goose, it's 'done for you.' Get it?"

"Got it," he said. "So, all right, I'm shutting up, but it can't last forever. What is it you're buttering me up for? What do you need? How much will it cost me?"

"Well, funny you should ask."

"What's funny about what I already know, and what I know is

that it will cost me a barrel of money or a bushel of something."

"Now, Gramps, just calm down. Take some deep breaths. And listen, please. We're using up cell phone minutes here, Gramps, wasting them, and that's money, and also green energy, buddy boy."

"I'm holding my breath, waiting for the axe to fall, but it's hard to talk when I'm holding my breath."

"I'll rescue you. I'll talk real fast. Gramps, I still want to come to Florida, and I will do all those things you are so proud of me doing, but, Gramps, when I come to enjoy the glories of Florida, I want to bring two other people. I want to bring Harriet."

"Harriet's good," Gramps said. "And? And? Speak up. Who broke my phone? Did the line go dead?"

"Harriet, and..."

"And?"

"Her brother."

"Her brother? Billy, that snot nosed fifteen-year-old? What? What is this? You're engaged to be married without telling me?"

"Gramps, calm down. It's nothing like that."

"Then what is it like? Is he your boyfriend? You wearing his fraternity pin?"

"Not really."

"Not really. I'm going to have a convulsion. I ask a simple question, 'Is he a boyfriend,' and I get a 'Not really'".

153

"Gramps, I'm thirteen years old. He is a boy and he is a friend, but he's not a boyfriend in the usual sense. You have all of that to look forward to."

"I hope your father and mother know about this pre-nuptial relationship you are having. I knew all this rabbit breeding was going to create problems."

"Gramps, of course they know and they are supporting the three of us coming together. They see him here every day. He's very, very good with the birds and very, very interested in helping with the mammals. You know, the furry ones."

"So that's the final definition of 'Not really'? That's all I get for all my concern and worries, 'not really'? Well, maybe half of him could fly to Florida and the other half not really get here. How do you like them apples?"

"Please Gramps. Try to see my side of it, for a change. Harriet's parents won't let her come unless he comes too. And if she doesn't come, I'll be very anxious on a big trip like that, flying by myself. And my dear, dear Cheap Grampa, don't tell me again how you came in steerage to Ellis Island all by yourself from the old country."

"Really, you don't want to hear about that again?"

"Well, not really, I mean, not just now. But sometime soon. I want to get this settled, first."

"Are their parents willing to pay their air fares?"

"Of course, Gramps."

"And money for pizzas, hot dogs and other beige foods?"

"Of course, Gramps."

"Money for all admissions, movies, county fairs, parking at all the beaches?"

"How could you doubt that?"

Grampa guffawed. "From past experience. But, ok, I'm feeling better now. Uh, oh, I just thought of something else. There will be a nominal twenty-four hour a day chaperone fee if the boy comes."

"Grampa, that's insulting. I can't tell Harriet and Billy's parents that there's a chaperone fee. And twenty-four hours a day?"

"What's the alternative? Should I put a leash on him? Or maybe a motion detector alarm? He's a boy isn't he?"

"Honest. Not really. Maybe next year. But right now, not really."

"Because you're the most honorable kid I know, and a pillar in our family, he can come, but he's got to agree to go with me on trash-day cruising, in case there's something heavy to lift."

"Now you're talking, Gramps. I'll agree for him. He's honorable, too. Thanks so much. Whoopee, we're going to have such a great time, my beloved Florida Grampa."

Then she sent a sweet kiss through the phone wires, and yelled, "Florida, here come the three of us."

Grampa grumbled. "And they'll take showers and use up my soap. Oh, well, it could have been four of them.

Grampa simply said, "Yes, really, you will."

Doctors

Grampa called Robin and she said, "How are you, Grampa?"

"I'm not sick."

"Well, that's good, but how do you know?"

He said, " The doctors told me so."

With that infinite patience, she said, "I know if I remain quiet for a while, you'll tell me what's going on."

"I don't want you to remain quiet," he said. "I love when you interrupt me, most of the time, of course, with your incredible wisdom. But the issue is I went to three doctors this week."

He could hear her soft anxiety. "Are you sick, Grampa? You have me worried. Why did you go to three doctors?"

"I told you, I'm not sick. It's just that time of year. Every October I do my annual thing. So first I went to the eye doctor."

Robin said, "You went to your optometrist. Yep, I learned that in seventh grade. What did he find out, Gramps?"

"It's not a he, you gender imperfect you, she's a she. And very, very dear."

"Whew, that relaxes me. But I hope I don't have to deal with you hitting on your doctor."

"Nah, she's only twenty years old."

Robin laughed. "Well, that's a relief."

"She's a professional. So she hands me this paddle and very politely she says, 'Cover your right eye and tell me, which of these two is better? One or two?'

"I always say, 'They look exactly alike.'

"'Now come on, sir,' she says, 'Switch the paddle, and cover the left eye. Which is better, one or two?'

"I grumble, and I mumble, 'They both look the same.'

"'Ok,' she says, 'What about these two? Which is clearer, two or three?'

"'Dear Dr. Optometrist,' I say, 'I'm not being difficult, they just both look alike. It's possible, isn't it?'"

"'Not for normal people, but Ok,' she says, cheerfully, 'We'll try another approach. Read these lines.'"

Grandpa said, "I do, I go through them like rain pouring down from the mountain, 'g4zytohiu2.'

"'Next line,' and I do that one, and then she says, 'Next line,' and I read it with only a few guesses."

"Grampa, you're not allowed to guess," Robin said. "This is serious. When I write my great novel I want you to be able to read every word, not guess at it."

Grandpa said, "For you, I'll get a big magnifying glass, but for her, I'll guess.

"Then the eye doctor young woman says, 'What, are you wearing sneaky contacts?'

"So, I says back to her, 'No, these are my eyes. I just eat a lot of carrots.'

157

"That's when she says, 'I give up. But, now to get even with you, I'm going to put these drops in. I know from last year, you hate them.'

"I open my mouth and she says, 'Quit complaining.'"

Robin said, "I would have bopped you on the head with the eye paddle."

Grandpa answered, "Well, I'm just glad you weren't there. And now I won't tell you that I swiped two copies of People Magazine for you and one for your Aunt Dee."

Robin said, "Thanks. I'll be good."

"Now, back to the doctor, who says, 'Put your chin on this chin rest, and now look at my ear.'

"I ask her, 'Why would I want to look at your ear? I'm a leg man, not an ear man.' She ignores me and says, 'Because I told you to, and I am a doctor.' And then, she blinds me with her light.

"'Now, the other eye.'

"I say, 'I can't see where the other ear is.' She gently pulls my nose until I'm back in the chin cup, and says, 'Look at my ear and no wise cracks,' and she blinds me again."

Robin said, "Oh, Grampa, grow up. She's doing her professional duty. What did she say next? Let me guess. 'Shut up and be good, mister'"

"That's just what she said. Were you there?" Grandpa sounded chagrined. "I'll grow up for next year's visit, but this is what she finally told me. Good news really.

"'Well, well, Sir,' she says. 'You don't have cataracts. You'll be able to drive at night for at least the next twenty years.' And then she does some kind of thing that checks the retina, a minor explosion. 'Well that checks out just fine. You keep your same glasses, and come see me next year, and we'll have more fun all over. But, do tell me what brand of carrots you eat. I want to recommend them to all my patients.'

"I shake her hand and say, 'Thanks, Doc. I'll look forward to it.' Then I write her a check for the co-pay, and make her hold the paddle over her left eye to see if the amount on the check was correctly written. She laughs and shoos me out. Someone else was waiting.

"And then I drive to the blood place. I had been fasting since midnight, so I couldn't eat until noon, when the appointment was scheduled. And the blood drawing is pleasant. I like going there, I always bring a jacket and walk out with two more copies of People Magazine for you and your aunt, and two old New Yorkers for me. The waiting room still has lots of Sports Illustrated and Woman's Day for the other customers. I don't feel at all immoral."

Robin said, "Well, I hope we won't get arrested for harboring hot merchandise."

Grampa laughed. "Well, two days later, I go to see my family doc, a good guy I've known for twenty years. We always start by my asking about his three sons. It's sort of an unstated counseling session, because one of the three is always in trouble of some sort and he seeks my wisdom, and I charge him a co-pay, just kidding, and we look at the blood work together. He comments on my blood pressure, which is 128 over 56. 'Not bad,' he says, 'for a teen-ager, and since you took yourself off the Lipitor, despite your great good cholesterol, the other numbers are high.'

"'Yeah, yeah,' I say, 'I'll probably die at the same time if I took the Lipitor or not.' And I remind him of the latest research on Statins, and give him a copy, that says the non-Statin people die more from violence and suicide than from heart attacks. He supports my Las Vegas health gambling attitude."

Robin said, "I'll keep you healthy by biking with you every chance I get, Grampa. And I'm sure if you keep buying cheap stuff, and just enough organics, you'll live for forever."

"Sounds like a deal," Grandpa answered. "And finally, that week, I go to the dentist, where I find out I have no cavities and all my wired teeth are sound. They do a cautionary x-ray, and my hygienist, whom I've known since she was a teen-ager, gives me the Flosser of the Month award."

"My sweet, sweet Grampa," Robin said, "I'm so proud of you. Tell me, Gramps, do you think I should give up being a marriage counselor and become a Doctor doctor, instead?"

Grandpa was silent for a little while, and then said, "I'd say, yes, honey, but only if all your patients were just like me, or at least as cute as ninth grade boys needing help."

"Now, there *you* got a deal, Gramps."

Transitions

His oldest son called on Christmas day, and brightened it immediately. One after another the grand kids got on the phone. The last one was the oldest one, Ani.

"Hi, Grampa. Merry Christmas."

"Merry Christmas, to you, too, Ani. And another hearty congratulation on your graduation."

"Thanks. I haven't told you yet which one I've decided to pick from the three presents you offered me. But I sure have read your note, over and over again. It made me feel great."

"You deserve to feel great. That was no small accomplishment, knocking off that MSW."

"Thanks, Grampa, and thanks for the absence of sarcasm about 'What took you so long?'"

"It never crossed my mind. And you sure had a lot on your mind, too. I wouldn't like to count all those trips out to Long Island to look in on your other grandparents. It was hard to hear that your grandma did die."

Ani simply said, "Thanks." And then added, "My other grampa has been through hell."

"Timing isn't always gracious, is it?"

"We do what we have to do."

"What's ahead now? To get a job? You and your guy thinking about marriage?"

She answered. "Yes, and yes, and maybe, maybe."

"I hear the signs of a woman in transition. Knowing you, it won't be stagnation, though. You'll know. And once you do, you'll move like a sky rocket, woman."

"The knowing isn't so easy, Grampa. Alternatives can be overwhelming."

"They're hard for almost everyone, Ani. So what are some alternatives staring you in the face? Mention a few, and we can get the ones you have no passion for out of the way."

"What if I have a passion for a lot of them, Gramps?"

"Then, we figure a way to clump them together, and if there isn't a job out there that uses our clump, we start writing a foundation grant to *make* such a job. Tell me a couple of the passions up for consideration."

"Well, I have to decide if I want to work in an agency or not. And if it's an agency, what kind, and where, and what kind of people will it serve?"

Grampa's only response was, "And?"

"That's funny, Grampa. One of my favorite professors said that every counselor could build a giant practice by keeping quiet, and really help more if he or she just kept asking, 'And?'"

"Very wise. And?"

"I never asked my prof where she had learned that technique, but it wouldn't surprise me if she had been one of your students."

"Maybe I also taught her to tell her clients to quit stalling and answer the question."

"All right, wise guy, and I know I want to work with underprivileged people."

Grampa smiled and even the telephone carried the smile, "No surprise, given what you've seen your mom and dad doing with their valuable lives."

"Yes, no surprise," Ani said. "But it's harder if I want to work in a New York City agency, not being an African-American. Not impossible. I was pretty well received at a couple of my internships, here in the city. But sometimes there was an edge when I walked into some agencies."

"That comes with the territory. Where do you stand on building a private practice? That precious MSW allows you to do third party billing, right?"

"Right, but, it also clarifies something. I wouldn't look forward to sitting in a room doing one on one counseling. Even counseling couples or families in an office."

"So?" he asked. "Did you notice how clever that word is, too?"

"Yes, Grampa, it was the second thing she taught me." They both laughed.

"So, I have to sort through the kind of agency I want to work with."

"Have you made a list? Child Welfare? Drug and Alcohol? Woman's Shelter?"

"Grampa, no wonder you got to be where you got to be. Yes, I need to make a list, and then start rank ordering the list, and then start networking to find out who's doing what out there."

"Oh, Ani, it's great listening to you and hearing your mind going clickity clack. You're at a wonderful place in your life. New beginnings. Being at the cutting edge of change. Finding opportunities for polishing your craft."

"You're making it a merrier Christmas, Grampa. Thanks for helping."

"Ani, you made my day, too. Just for the record, the only Christmas present you get from your Cheap Grampa is 'help.' It's three times the adventure at one third the cost for me."

"Yeah, yeah. All of us kids are wise to you and this pretense of being cheap. Look what I got to face: Which of the graduation presents am I going to choose from among these alternatives? 1. The imitation mink stole including its moths and probably fleas. 2. The trip next Christmas by freighter to Poland. And 3. One raffle ticket, probably competing with twenty other tickets out there, on your 1991 Toyota."

"Well, life is full of transitions, Ani. I'm mailing you one of my favorite books, and in it is a chapter on a strategy called 'The Planning Board.' It's something that can help anyone figure out what they really, really, *really* want to do."

"Well, thanks, Grampa. My favorite teacher already taught all of us about The Planning Board. Was that really, truly, yours?"

"Yep. It just goes to show, we got to hang out more together."

All she said was, "And? So?"

And all he said was, "I got it. It'll give me something to look forward to in the New Year. Thanks. Merry Christmas, dear, dear granddaughter. And my love to all the people you love, some I just happen to know, and that includes all the dogs, too. I love you. Merry Christmas."

Being Taken In

Grampa got a call from Ani, the oldest of the granddaughters. She was in her apartment in New York City. He was surprised to get a second call so soon after yesterday's.

"Hey, how great you called. What's up, Ani? Any luck with the job search?"

"That's one of the reasons I wanted to call. Your letter of recommendation really helped. You won't believe this, but one of your old graduate students runs the agency. Nancy Clarkson."

"Oh, Ani, you got a job at the Harry Chapin Food Bank?"

"That's the one."

"Congratulations. She's a winner. You picked smart, kid, but of course, she picked the smartest. She got you."

She laughed. "Well, as you always say, 'we'll see.' The fit seems perfect, and I'm excited to be there. But, listen, Gramps, I also called about this thing I heard from the other kids that you've been talking about old people having to be taken in by their kids. I don't see you as old, so what gives?"

Now it was his turn to laugh. "You're right. Oh, occasionally I pour the orange juice from the juice container into my coffee, but not every morning. But a lot of the other guys on the Island are doing the bigger things, like frying their frying pans and leaving the showers on all night. And the kids have come and are picking them off, one by one."

She said, "Oh, boy, then the rotating thing starts. The oldest daughter gets him for a month, until her family gets bored, and then she rotates him to the oldest son and his family, until Grampa gets bored, and they hold the great family lottery to see who gets him next."

"It ain't pretty. The grampa...."

She interrupted, "Or the grandma, because the women get caught up in it, too. Often, I learned in one of my courses, she outlives grampa, and she's older and frequently more fragile, even less able to take care of herself."

"Oh, yeah," he said, "I've seen it down here a lot. The old folks always have a suitcase packed, with the extra tooth brush and denture cleaner in it, ready to go."

Ani said, "I want you to know, that when you get to be about a hundred and ten, I'll be ready to be in the rotation, Gramps."

"Thanks. Just what I needed to know. Your charming aunt up in Vermont, has promised that they will give me a nice tent out in their vegetable garden. 'Right between the broccoli and the Brussel sprouts.' I had to remind her: 'not too close to the poison ivy, please.'"

Ani said, "Well, that will work for summers, but our old house in Ithaca has the most wonderful wood stove you can curl up close to every winter."

"Is your other grandad thinking of moving up there? How's he doing without your grandma? Man, it can get lonely."

"Well, he really had two years or more of tough caretaking before she died. He's doing a lot of resting. And catching up. He put a lot of things on the back burners. His art work, for instance. He's starting to do more and more of it. And that takes him back out into the community. They made a lot of friends there. He's not so ready to move."

"The older I get, the more of the friends I outlive. I get nervous when the phone rings. Yours is the first cheery one today. A lot of the calls tell me of the change of address of an old friend.

The new address is usually to some nursing home. That's the rhythm of it, Ani. You live for years in some place, then, as you get old, you get rotated. And then, when that gets too hard on the families, you get nursing homed. It's the next to last place."

"All right, sour puss. Don't go there. I know the implication of the 'last place.' But the way you take care of yourself, I figure you got another twenty-five years. Hell, some of your kids will be ready for the assisted living before you."

"Good, then I can put some of them in the tent out between the broccoli and the Brussels sprouts."

She laughed. "And not too close to the poison ivy. Thanks again, Gramps, for the recommendation letter. It made all the difference."

"So do you, Ani. So do you. Good luck in all that's ahead. And thanks for calling. Please do it soon again. I take my cell phone with me out to the Brussel sprouts."

Fire

The phone rang. Grampa's caller ID told him who it was. He picked up and started yelling. "No, I'm not buying anything. Just give me *your* phone number and I'll call you during your dinner tomorrow night. Don't argue with me. Don't call me, I'll call you."

He made no move to hang up, but asked, "Are you still there, honey bunch?" It was his granddaughter. She got most of his jokes, first draft, right out of the fire.

"Oh, Grampa, what if that was a real person, not just me, and you spoke like that?"

"Well, maybe they wouldn't call me back again. And since you are one of my favorite real persons, I'm glad you didn't hang up on me. What are you doing? What made you call? And boy, I'm glad you did. I was going to call you."

"Well, I called to find out how you're doing. I miss you. So, what was one of your high points so far today?"

"I love when you do that," he said. "And you never fail. I believe you truly care."

"Of course I care, so tell me. High point? Move it, Buster."

"Well, funny you should ask. I was out in the back. I built myself a fire in the fire pit."

She laughed. "Did you bring out some marshmallows on a coat hanger wire?"

"You mean, like we did when you and I built the fire on the beach down here in Florida, before someone called the cops on us because we didn't have a fire permit?"

"Oh, I remember. The officer expected to find a bunch of drunken college kids or something. Not two gray haired old grandparents, an emerging teenager and her uncle and aunt with a three month old baby."

"Mostly, he didn't know what to do with a grandma strumming on her guitar and all of us singing, 'This Land Is Your Land...' Do you remember what he said?"

"Oh, I do. He was a good guy. He got it. I remember he said, 'Make sure you put out all the fire, cover it with sand, and next time, please, get a permit, so if someone calls in and squeals on you, we can tell them, 'They got a permit. They're a family, famous Country Western singers from Nashville. Good night, folks, but, by any chance, would you mind singing Woody's song, 'I'm On The Road Again' as I leave you and get back on the road again?'"

"And Grandma did sing it. Oh, I remember, we all laughed so hard, even the baby joined in."

Grampa said, "We done good. Hey, and now your highpoint?"

"Well, it's still early, and calling you usually gives me at least one I can report when my mom asks me about my highpoint."

"Nothing else?"

"Well, now that you asked, I'm making something for my mom for her birthday. It's going to be a macrame necklace. Don't tell her. It's going to be a secret."

"Damn, I was going to make her a macrame necklace, myself. Do you think she would want two? Or I could make her a choker? How about a set of macrame earrings to match your necklace."

"That would be great," Phoebe said. "Do I need to send you some yarn?"

169

"Hey, it's Cheap Grampa you're talking to, and I can send you some yarn. I buy it at yard sales. I have a bushel of it. How's your stock?" And they both laughed.

"But, listen, did your mom ever tell you what your grandma and I used to do for her birthday when she was little? I mean 52 years ago, the years we all lived right near the beach on Long Island."

"What did you do, take her out fishing for whales? You know how I feel about hurting wild life. No? Ok, tell me."

"The fire I made tonight reminded me of it as I was sitting there cooking my salmon on the grill. The salmon made me think of you, too. I know it's your favorite. But we threw a big party on the beach out there. She invited lots of kids, and for the two months before, I kept collecting big driftwood logs and I threw them up on the dunes, until I knew I had enough for a gigantic fire worthy of your mom's birthday. It would take a whole squad of police to break up that fire or the whole party."

Phoebe said, "You'd be able to convince whatever law guys came that this was a party worth joining. And Grandma had her guitar, right?"

"Oh, yeah and song sheets all printed out for everyone, even the ones too little to read. And there were lots of neighbors keeping anyone from falling into the fire."

She suddenly grew silent. And then said, "I wish I could have been there."

"Say," Grampa said, "When you come back down to Florida in January, we'll throw a party like that for you on the beach. Yeah, I know your birthday isn't in January. We just won't mention that to the police when they come. Oh, and Phoebe, there was one other thing about the birthday parties for your mom."

"What, you bought her a reduced for quick sale, two days old birthday cake from the used bakery store? Just kidding. Tell me, what was the other thing. This I got to imagine, amidst a bonfire the size of Radio City Music Hall, and all those kids singing. But, hurry up, I got cages to clean and birds and squirrels to feed."

"Well, this is good. Listen, and then you can go to work. Each kid had to dig a shallow hole in the sand about the size of a small pie plate. I had sample pie plates as guides, and the neighbors helped. Then the kids had to fill the hole, on their own, with shells, and sea weed, feathers, drift wood hunks, anything they could find. They combed that beach up and down, and my job in the meantime was to mix up plaster in a bunch of buckets, and whenever a kid was done, I'd pour the plaster over their hole, and they used a stick to smooth it off."

She said, "I can picture that. And then what happened?"

"Well, that's when we moved over to another part of the beach and had the cookout and more songs. They toasted their own marshmallows on coat hanger wires, and only five or six kids got burned, no just kidding, only some of the marshmallows got really burned, but the good ones turned into the best s'mores anyone ever ate."

She laughed, and said, "And when eating was done, I bet you had it figured out that the plaster would be dry and hard, so they could each take home their gift from the sea."

"Whoa, that's pretty poetic, and exactly right. But would tomorrow be inconvenient to fly down so we can practice making fires and not get caught?"

"No, Gramps, too much else to do tomorrow. Thanks, and I love you, just for who you are. My grampa. Gotta go."

"Love you, thanks for calling, Don't eat any plaster hot dogs."

ALBUM EIGHT
REMINISCENCES

Looking Back To Pocusset Street

It was the Family Reunion week. The badminton court that morning had ten people playing, with two shuttlecocks in the air at the same time, and a couple of little kids on bigger one's shoulders and no one trying to win. Not at badminton, or anything else, either. That's the kind of kids they were. Good kids. Grampa's kind of kids.

Breakfast had been corn fritters, the corn leftover from last night's corn on the cob, lovingly fried in coconut oil, prescribed by their Aunt Dee, family nutritionist and karate teacher. Grampa had brought over some boysenberry syrup, that grandson Jay, the film maker, had taken the time to read the use-by date.

"Grampa," he said, "I know you're cheap, but this stuff goes back to the black and white silent films of Cecil B. DeMille."

He came over to Grampa and gave him a big hug. "Just kidding. And listen, Gramps. The Ithaca branch is going to steal you away this afternoon. We've organized a trip to someplace just for you, and no one else but us can go. And I'm going to make a movie about it. It's a project, and if I don't get it done, I don't graduate."

"What, I should now be guilty if you don't graduate?"

Robin, who *had* just graduated college, came over and put her arms around Grampa, too. And said, "No, Grampa, you're just necessary to the adventure and film. And I've made some of your famous provolone wrapped around smoked salmon, stuffed with pecans and bright orange apricots rollups for all of us. That's going to be lunch."

Lark, the fifteen-year-old said, "And, Gramps, I'm in charge of dessert, of course, and I went to Herrells and we have here three quarts of the finest flavors they make. Starting with kumquat fudge." Grampa gave her a big hug, and said, "My favorite. Oh, you know a way to a grampa's heart, you always did, great seeker of premium ice cream. I hope it was a buy one get one, and I pray it's just a little out of date."

"Sorry, Gramps. You know Herrells. You buy premium, you pay premium. I took out a loan at the bank before I went in."

Ani, the oldest of the kids, the one who had also just graduated, earning a coveted Master of Social Work degree, came over and hugged him, too, and said, "I'm in charge of the program for the afternoon. And I want to remind everyone that when I called Cheap Grampa to tell him I had just got my degree, he didn't say, 'Congratulations' or anything like that, he just said, 'Great, now you can get third party payments.'"

Grampa laughed, hard, and said, "I did not. Although it crossed my mind. I did say, 'I have three wonderful presents for you for graduating, but you have to rank order them and you only get to choose one of them.' Ho ho."

Ani said, "Oy, what presents. One was a ticket for a freighter that would take me to Poland in the middle of the winter, and I couldn't even bring my dog along."

Grampa, sounding a little defensive said, "But I told you, you could bring your boyfriend with you as long as he paid his own way."

They all laughed and Ani said, "Ok, where's your car, we're ready to go. We're going to blindfold you, and you only can take the blindfold off when we get there. We all remember you taking us on an adventure, and we had to each wear a blindfold."

Grampa said, "That's the way it goes. Three times the adventure at one third the cost."

"But, Grampa," they all said in chorus, "Did we really have to eat all those speckled, over-ripe brown bananas?"

Grampa laughed loud and hard. "They were reduced for quick sale, as always, and anyhow, I wanted you to wait to find out, years later, that bananas were really yellow, in case you ever decided to compete on Jeopardy."

Jay said, "Yeah. To keep us safe from bananas, I'm driving, and yes, I have a license. And also, yes, I've wanted to drive that old Toyota of yours for years, and now is my chance, oh blindfolded one." The laughter that rose was music in Grampa's ears.

Jay added, "I brought this tape recorder along. So whatever any of you say that's brilliant enough, I just might build into the movie." Everyone shouted, "Bravo, Brava."

They all got into the car, and pulled Grampa, blindfolded, into the back between Lark and Robin. Ani rode up front with Jay, so she could read the Garmin, turn on the tape recorder, and boss Jay around.

Grampa started to get his excited happy anticipation look on. He asked, "Did you bring water, and napkins? I got an ice cream scooper, you remember, in the glove compartment."

Robin said, "We thought of everything, Grampa. Even poison ivy lotion for when we leave you out in the poison ivy patch. Just kidding."

Ani, in charge, said, "Now, Grampa, what this is all about is we want to hear everything we can today, about your childhood. What it was like growing up in your neighborhood. What kinds of things did you do to just play when you were a kid?"

Robin added, "They all read the interview I did with you. So we all know the gloomy stuff about the boarding house. And, yes, it wasn't all gloomy. We know about your cookie person,

Ms. Watterson, and about Alfie and you getting that great preschool education, and being taken to the Carnegie Library on Friday's. Able to bring into your house the first books that were ever in there. But we brain-stormed some other questions, and Ani has them. Let's get going."

Jay started up the old Toyota convertible. It rattled and shook, and when Jay spoke he imitated Grampa so well they thought it *was* Grampa. "All right, everyone of you. Pay attention. Get your seat belts on and fasten your helmets. No smoking of anything, and everyone, start riding shotgun. There are a lot of nuts on the road. Not only do I want you to live long lives, but I don't want any dents in my Toyota. I'm still making payments."

Jay made them all laugh. Lark said, "Grampa, we all know the car is really paid for, so just relax, man, and enjoy us."

He said, "I do. You kids are one of my all time great joys in my otherwise overjoyed life."

Ani, said, "Thanks, Mistah. Now I have the first question. We know you grew up in Pittsburgh. Lived on Pocusset Street. The house had six bedrooms. Woods were all around it. What was the neighborhood like?"

"It wasn't classy. But, it wasn't in a slum, either. This is interesting. We were all either Catholics or Jews. There were no Protestants. Isn't that amazing? I honestly didn't know there was anything called a Protestant until high school!"

Jay asked, "What? That's amazing. Hmm. Were the Catholics Irish?"

Grampa answered. "No, interestingly enough. We had a lot of Italians, and boy, could they play baseball. And there were three families, related to each other, of Syrian Catholics. There were a lot more Jews. Are you ready for this? Our high school cancelled school on Yom Kippur. Really. No one would come. The Italians took it as a snow day. Ho ho."

Robin asked, "Were there any conflicts on that street?"

"None at all. We kids all got along. Played a lot of softball, on an empty lot. The bigger kids had helped clear it, years before. And this is interesting. When we showed up, one kid brought the old ball, all taped up and re-taped each game. Another had the one bat, and one big kid brought a crow bar."

"A crow bar?" Jay asked.

"Yeah," Grampa answered. "For when the ball got foul tipped over the head of the catcher and went down the street into the sewer. That's when I was glad my best friend, Alfie, was smaller than I was. When the manhole cover was crowbarred off, two bigger guys held him by his ankles and lowered Alfie into the sewer to fetch the ball. And the game continued.

"We started playing very young. Began by just running bases, and later we got positions, three or four of us in right field, or backing up the catcher. We played all day in the summer, even after supper we came back and played more. There was an annual World Series against Melvin Street, and they lost every year. They didn't have as many Italians."

Ani asked, "What else did you do for fun?"

Grampa answered. "On summer nights, when it got dark, we played hour after hour of kick the can, until the mothers called everyone in. We weren't sexist. Girls played kick the can, too. One of the girls had a Monopoly game, and we played that a lot. Cards, too. Hearts, mostly, until one of the guys organized strip poker, over on the Monopoly girl's screened-in back porch. Until we got caught.

"Every summer we had a Lawn Fete. Sort of a block party that had home-made games of chance: dart throwing, fishing in a bucket, a home-made roulette wheel. Amazing, without much adult supervision we included everyone, and little kids had little booths, and some of the older kids set up a haunted house. I remember one of the parents called the newspaper and we all had our picture in the paper. Most of us for the first time. We raised money for poor children.

"Once summer was over, and school started, we played touch football on the street, endlessly, until it got dark. Or for me, until I went to deliver on my paper route."

Robin said, "Oh, Gramps, no wonder you grew up cheap. You worked hard. I remember, you also delivered for a pharmacy a couple of nights every week. Got home at 10 p.m."

Grampa added, "But with lots of tip money. I didn't get an allowance, bought all my own clothes, and stuff."

Ani told Jay. "It's the next right hand turn, Jay, about two miles down. And we'll be there. Grampa, tell us about when girls came into your life?"

Grampa laughed. "You mean in third grade where I went to the first party where they played 'Spin the bottle?'"

Jay said, "We all have to start somewhere."

"This has been wonderful, kids. Such memories come roaring back. Can I tell you one last one and maybe you can take this blindfold off."

"Not yet, Gramps," Ani said. "Hang in there. Jay, find a parking place when we get there. Might take longer than the whole journey. Ok? Now Gramps, what did you want to tell us?"

"Again, this has been so sweet for me. Thanks, all of you. Well, the memory came flashing back. Of girls."

Lark said, "This isn't X rated is it, Grampa? I may have get my hall pass signed by my mom."

"No, no. This is clean as a Pocusset Street whistle. We were in the seventh grade, and one of the great girls on the street decided, after school, on rainy days, when there was no touch football, she would teach us how to dance."

Robin said, "How sweet. I can see it. This was before TV, and probably still in the Depression. Your hard working parents didn't dance much, I guess, so this wise girl knew there was no other place you would learn it."

"Right," Grampa said. "Her name was Ann Sirota, and they had a finished basement. Pretty ritzy. She had a record player and records. Again, pretty ritzy.

"I couldn't wait for a rainy day. Ann never criticized. Amazing how she instinctively knew that. Encouraged even the clumsiest among us. And I wasn't clumsy. I was born to dance. And Ann taught us well. I remember the coal stoker would come in, and too often in the middle of a Glenn Miller slow song."

Ani, the good counselor said, "And?"

"And, well, Ann got us all ready for the great season of Bar Mitzvahs. For which the Synagogue (reformed type), had a dance almost every Saturday night."

Jay announced. "Well, that probably kept you out of the saloons, Grampa."

"It was a different time. I don't remember that alcohol was ever part of the scene, back then. Certainly, no drugs. No one had the money for any of that stuff."

Robin said, "Sounds idyllic, Gramps. I love your stories. But, oh, look, gang. It looks like we're here. Ok to take off his blindfold, Ani? And Jay, get your movie camera ready."

Ani said, "Are you ready Grampa? Surprise, surprise, Grampa. I'll count to three. A perfect surprise for our cheapest, sweetest, dearest Grampa."

They had taken him to the little urban pocket park right across from his favorite store of all stores. Aptly named "Deals and Steals." Where nothing is sold that isn't out of date, bruised, or reduced for quick sale, and all bananas are speckled brown. Its signature special is "All Chips. All Types. All buy-one-get-two free."

Grampa's eyes got misty. All he could say was: "This is 'poifect.' Absolutely 'poifect.' Thanks sooo much, you kids. I feel so lucky, so privileged. And just like it was for your dad, when he was a kid, on allowance day, you each get some money to spend. One cent more than your age. And I got the change right here in my zippered purse. They don't call me big-spender for nothing."

"Oh, Grampa. Grampa, Grampa, Grampa," and everybody hugged everybody, right there on the sidewalk.

Ideas About Birthday Presents

Cheap Grampa had several ideas for birthdays, not one of which required the spending of money. To Cheap Grampa, the damn things kept coming around year after year, and for what? Just more contributions to the buy-me-gimme generation of kids who already had all the violent computer games you could squeeze into one game room. They had more t-shirts than they could ever wear, and water guns, bicycles, hot air balloons, laser blinders and more dirty movies than they would ever watch before they grew out of PG 13.

When the kids were younger, Cheap Grampa would nail together some hand-made things. Back when orange crates were wood, he'd find an old pair of roller skates and bang together a scooter for a present that the other kids on the block would laugh at, and Cheap Grampa would say, "Go get your manufactured scooter, Snot Nose, and we'll race." And by gum, Grampa's orange crate scooter won race after race.

He made a lot of jewelry for the girls out of beer caps, and he put together pillows he sewed up from bandanas stuffed with shipping popcorn. He made photographic pencil-holders out of soup cans, and scotch taped their favorite pictures around the can.

The kids were tolerant. Cheap Grampa had other virtues, so they overlooked his cheapness. They did draw the line, however, when he wanted to make them a birthday morning omelet out of road-kill chipmunks he found out on the highway.

His own kids, now the parents of all the grand kids, just rolled their eyes, and mumbled, "What can we do with him? We ain't going to change him, that's for sure. Poor thing, raised in the Great Depression, he probably never had a real birthday party of his own back then. No wonder he convinced Mom to do that thing about our birthdays, at least until we got old enough to say, 'Enough is enough, dad.'

"You know what I mean. That thing he had us print on all of our birthday party invitations." Cheap Grampa's kids all groaned in chorus. "Yeah, yeah. That famous sentence: 'No bought presents will be allowed. Only homemade presents will be acceptable.'"

"You could see the whole neighborhood's lights on way past midnight, as those compliant neighbors stayed up all night gluing and painting and cutting and sewing and doing something that we all pretended had been made by the kids themselves. The spirited competition was fun to look back on.

"So, listen all of you. Let's plan a birthday for Cheap Grampa, and that's just what we'll do. I can see it now. I can hear him complaining. 'You cheap skates. After all I haven't done for you.'"

And that's just what we did. Oh, what an event it was. He cried all through it. At the homemade mobiles everyone made for him. Some of us used beer cans. Others drilled holes in shells they had gathered right from his own beach. One of the sisters made one from old stuffed animals, taken right out of his "Possible Presents Closet." He must have bought them forty years ago for us kids.

His oldest son made a mobile from framed butterflies. And Grampa kept on crying all through the present opening, and then he picked up his old three string guitar and we sang like crazy, all night, until the full moon came up, and since Cheap Grampa only eats ice cream on the full moon, we all really indulged, and indulged some more, since the ice cream for sure was something he had bought on the buy one get one sale.

He made us all sign a petition against the ice cream companies that had abandoned what used to be half gallons in favor of forty-eight ounces. We took up our own guitars then, and played while he thanked us for the birthday party he had always wanted, with real birthday presents, hand made with love.

Cheap Grampa And The Cruise Ship

On one of his visits to Ithaca, Cheap Grampa picked up his ninth grade granddaughter after school. She waved wildly when she saw his car, and immediately dragged over two overly embarrassed teen boys she had been talking to, up by the entrance to the school.

"This is that famous Grampa of mine I have been telling you about. Gramps, this is Fred, and the red headed one is Red. Guys, this is Cheap Grampa."

Grampa shook their hands, firmly, and said, "You boys have good taste in women. This woman is destined for greatness," which embarrassed them more, which, of course, was his intent.

"Well, we know that," both of them said almost in chorus, eager to get away.

Grampa waved them a dismissive good bye. "I urge you not to forget that. Ok, Lark, let's get going. Times a wasting. We have an adventure ahead."

To the boys she said, "Don't take him too seriously, guys. He lives by something called 'Three times the adventure at one third the cost.' We love him, this Cheap Grampa. See you tomorrow, I'll tell you all about it." The boys faded away and she hopped into the car, giving them a quick, "Don't take any wooden nickels, guys."

"Oh, my darling granddaughter, it is clear you are one of the breed."

"Yep, I am Grampa, and one of the best. I also know all the bad family joke lines."

"Boy, do I know that. Like this joke of going with me this afternoon to give a look at this old age home your mom recommended."

Lark reached out and touched his hand that was on the steering wheel. "And we all know that it's about fifty years away when you might need a joint like that. Mom wants you to look at it as much for her own dad."

"Your dad told me. Whew. I count myself lucky. But, back to our mission. Here's the directions. You ride shotgun and tell me where to turn off the Pike. By the way, did you have a good day at school?"

"Oh, Grampa, yes, I did. I love this school. Particularly the Latin Studies teacher, who is also my home room teacher. She truly knows what she's doing, and all of us can barely wait for that period, even though the other ones are pretty great, too."

He smiled, "I so remember your graduation night from eighth grade. The whole celebration made me a believer. But, hey, I've got to talk to you before we get to this joint." He pulled over, and strangely enough, there was an ice cream place that just happened to be there, one he knew, one about a mile beyond where they were to turn off, but shotgun had her mind elsewhere, and the ice cream store may have manifested itself from her wishes. She was a family champ on good ice cream.

"Oh, Grampa, are we really stopping? How did you know I was aching for some ice cream?"

"Easy, I've seen your aches before. Now, me, I'm not having dessert until after dinner, but I'll get you something small, so you'll listen to what I have to say. Is that a deal?"

"Of course. I know this place. I'll get one scoop and two spoons. How's that for cheap?"

"Because you're so reasonable, brilliant, charming, and honorable, I say, out of the goodness of my cheap heart, you get two scoops and one spoon. Honest. That's my request. It's a long thing I have to talk about. And you need to eat the stuff slowly, slowly."

When Grampa pulled into a parking place, way out in right field, as far away from the door as possible, Lark kissed him on the cheek and got out. He reached into his wallet and gave her a Monopoly $5 bill. It was an old family joke. And she gave him back the old punch line.

"You go right to jail, do not pass 'Go' and please give me a real $5 bill. I'll bring you back the change, but hey, Gramps, if they have kumquat fudge, I'm getting you one scoop and two spoons and maybe you'll give me a bite."

He laughed. They both knew they never have kumquat fudge, even though every time he's at any ice cream store he asks them for that flavor.

"Thanks a lot, oh generous one."

"No problemo," she said. "I'm practicing my Español."

As she walked away, he admired her poise and strength. He wasn't kidding when he told her boys that she was destined for greatness. She wasn't gone long, and she had about five paper napkins and a most satisfactory dish of blueish ice cream. She was an ice cream gourmet.

"Quit staring. It's blueberry fudge. You should have seen the look she gave me when I asked, 'If you can make blueberry fudge, how come you can't make kumquat fudge?'"

"Thanks for caring, honey, and you always do." She held out a spoonful of ice cream to him. "No thanks, I'll pass on fudgey blueberries, and anyhow, just listen now. I've a story I want to tell you. You can interrupt any time you want. Just eat slowly, it's long and important." He cleared his throat and began telling his story. She ate slowly. He smelled the blueberries, more than the fudge.

"I am the Captain of my destiny. That's the point of my story. And since I was in the navy, I'm certain I can be captain of my own cruise ship. Now, normally a cruise ship would not be something you would think a Cheap Grampa would know anything about."

Lark interrupted, softly. "I think I remember hearing some rumors. You're going good, Gramps."

"Thanks. I'm sure you heard some of this. Now back to my story. When your grandma went through a tough time, that bout with the hair-bite of dementia, there were heavy pressures to put her in a nursing home. My cheap kids all rallied and had a little contest to see who could find the cheapest nursing home. I voted, of course, to keep her home.

"My daughter protested, loudly, at that time. 'Dad, listen. You barely change your own underwear and to put you in charge of her underwear? And, my dearest father, when was the last time you bathed her? I bet you don't even know what temperature she'd want her bath.'"

Lark laughed. "Oops, she got you there, Gramps, but if it's any comfort, it would have gotten me, too. I can't imagine bathing my mother."

"Let's hope you'll never have to, but I know you, if you have to, you will. Now, let me finish storytelling."

She licked her empty spoon, put another tiny bite on it, and listened.

"One of the tricky things for the kids was, if they found the cheapest nursing home near them, it would mean having to move both of us out their way. Not such a bad deal to have their mother close enough to visit, but what about having to put up with me. They could all imagine that, ho ho, and much too loudly, too clearly.

"They started to tease me about things I'd probably say: 'Do you have to use real butter in this house? How much dish detergent do you have to put in to wash one lousy frying pan. Turn off that air conditioner. I can live in a jungle and never sweat.'

"Quickly, one by one, they reported, mentioning very high costs for all the nursing homes in their area. And each asked me to check out the rates where we lived. I did, and they all breathed easier. 'Pop, you're living in Bargainsville. Yours is the cheapest of anything the four of us have found.' They were all taught to be honest, but I could hear them all lying like they worked for General Electric.

"So, that's when I booked the first cruise. Just think of it. For $750 bucks a week, we had all of our meals cooked, and dishes and pots washed. I could soak in the hot tubs. They had a doctor on board. Nurses, too. And what if she couldn't remember what she had seen at the evening nightclub shows, she sat through them, grinning the whole night away. We could sit in deck chairs. People would pass by and visit. She was charming, up and until they asked her how many children she had, and when they saw her blank face, they would gently slink away. But, with eight hundred passengers, there were always new Samaritans going by.

"She dressed up for Mexican night and remembered to say ' buon giorno,' and 'guten abend' all through French night."

Lark laughed. "I could have helped her Mexican night all right. Oh well. Go ahead, Gramps. I was too young to know all that. This is fascinating."

"I'll bring the pictures to show you, sometime, honey. We had a great time. I could play canasta or read up in a beach chair when she took her afternoon naps, which often lasted five hours. She took all her meds, because everything was easy. No one dropped in on us. We could call the kids and back-home friends from our cabin and report that everything was just fine. And cheap. They don't call me Cheap Grampa for nothing. The cheapest nursing home was $1,500 a week. Need I remind you, that's all the cruise ship charged. For both of us."

Lark put her spoon down and reached across and gave him a giant hug. And she said, "So, I figure, when it's your time, fifty years from now, of course, we would just keep booking cruise ship passages for you. You know what, Grampa, I'll take charge of that, in case you forget. I'll be sixty-six years old then, and I can come with you. Right?"

"Not only right, but poifect, and your grand kids can come visit us in Cancun. It seems all cruise ships stop there, coming or going. I have such good memories of that time. Incidentally, I kept winning at Canasta. And oh, the food. 'Weren't the cooking good?'"

Lark finished the sentence, just one of the family jokes, "And just bushels of it, too."

They both laughed. Lark hugged him again. "I wish Grandma was still here. I barely knew her."

"Thanks honey. She would have loved you. Destiny is destiny. She gave it her best shot."

"I saved the last spoonful for you, Gramps."

"Thanks, honey, but no thanks. I'm the captain of my destiny, and also the captain of this waistline. Ahoy, matey. Let's get to the cruise line. Oops, I mean, the nursing home."

"Ay, ay, mi Capitano."

Thanks

"Oh, Robin, I wish you had known my father, your great grandfather."

"Was he cheap like you, Grampa?"

"Funny enough, he was cheap, but he didn't like it as much as I do."

"Well, let's face it Gramps, nobody likes it as much as you."

"Thanks for noticing, woman. But his cheapness came out of necessity, trying to support a family during the Great Depression. I'm embarrassed that I haven't told you much about him."

"I'd love to learn more about him. Maybe you can fill me in when we have our picnic lunch down by the river. And it's also stuff I want to know for the upcoming 'Big Interview.'" Grampa nodded an agreement and Robin noticed he had teared up a little, as he often did when he remembered things that were tender.

"He probably never ever had a picnic by a river in his entire life, Robin."

"What, were they not invented yet when he lived?"

"Oh, yes, they were invented, just not available for everyone. He worked six and a half days of every week as long as he lived. That doesn't give you a lot of time for picnics.

"He packed a sandwich every day for lunch. And he had a thermos bottle of hot tea. And my mother managed to convince him of the value of an apple for dessert.

"Wow, the memories come flying back. There were two times in every year when he took me along to work with him."

"You did tell me once what his job was, Grampa. He drove a truck, right? And he would drive to small tailor shops and pick up their bundles of stuff for dry cleaning? Right?"

"You got it honey. And the two busiest times of the year for dry cleaning were just before Christmas and just before Easter. That's when I worked. And what fun it was. Every tailor shop we went to, they were glad to see him. He was a jolly man, with a joke or story on his lips, so friendly, and he remembered their kids, asked questions and always had something nice to say about everybody."

Robin laughed. "That's funny, I say the same things about you."

Grampa looked a little shy. "Thanks, honey. That's a very nice thing to tell me."

"It's true, Gramps."

They turned into the road that took them down to the river, double checked their brakes, and stopped down at the dock just before going into the river, hopped off, and started to unload lunch.

Grampa made an announcement. "Today's picnic lunch is brought to you by the Pilgrims from Plymouth Plantation. It's turkey. And don't bother to make any complaints that this is the fifth day in a row you are eating turkey sandwiches. It was a big bird and I've frozen sandwich meat for the next month."

Robin said. "I don't mind the same thing in a row, Grampa. I do like that you slip a few cranberries in a sandwich every now and then."

"And did you notice, occasionally, there are a few frozen peaches from the drops from last summer, and every now and then, a few blueberries, still blue from our trip to the Adirondacks over Labor Day."

"Yep, I've noticed. Look at my blue teeth from yesterday's blueberries."

She smiled, but they weren't blue, not her perfect teeth. "Now, back to Great Grampa."

"Well, mentioning Thanksgiving tickles some memories. We always celebrated his birthday at Thanksgiving. The real date was the twenty-ninth of November, but he brought extra fun to every Thanksgiving when we saved money by combining the holidays. One turkey, twice the fun, is my motto."

Then Grampa got silent. "There was one Thanksgiving, before he died. He had been living in the nursing home, and we checked him out for the weekend. All of us got all of our kids and as much extended family as we could, to get to Pittsburgh for the biggest party of them all. We knew it might be his last.

"Oh, there was turkey and pumpkin pies and all the rest. But the biggest thing of all was the thanking part of Thanksgiving.

"We set Great Grandpa up on a chair where he sat on four pillows, like a throne, and he sat, grinning down at all of us. Someone made him a crown, and we put a Superman cape on him, and for about two hours, guess what we did?"

Robin said, "I know it wasn't a roast, Grampa."

"No, honey, it was a toast. Everyone, one after the other, thanked him. Some of it was in stories, some of it in poems they had written and then read to him. There were a couple of funny skits, and several songs, changing the lyrics to tell something wonderful about him."

"It must have been so tender."

"It was, honey. Tender, and funny and full of his wisdom, reflected back to him. Tears were abundant, that's for sure. It was so impressive to see people be vulnerable to their feelings. Little kids telling him how they loved him, and reminding him of trips to the merry-go-round, and popsicles behind Granma's back. And catching baseball with him, flying kites, his jokes and his stories.

"The sum total was that everyone got to say to him what they might have said at a funeral. But this was the real memorial, because he said thanks, thanks, thanks, right back at them."

Robin, reached out and took Grampa's hand. "What a wonderful thing it must have been. I so wish I could have been there. And it didn't cost a penny, did it, Gramps? Maybe we'll do the same thing for you, but not for at least forty more years."

"Knowing you, you'll fill me with more thank you's than anybody else. And I know I'll cry, but I can take it. It's such a bargain."

Cheap Grampa, Lark and Moms

Another morning, after everyone slept late on a Saturday, Grampa and Lark, that fifteen-year-old granddaughter, were out on the bike path again. She busily greeted all dog owners and admired their mutts. Grampa continued his policy of dutifully ignoring anyone not wearing a helmet who said, "Hello" to them.

And Lark noted that he was dangerously close to moving into lecture mode. Lark was one of his favorite audiences. He said, "Over this long and dusty road, Lark, I have witnessed moms in action. Most of them glorious, and only a few inglorious. Take the one who walloped the kid who knocked over the pasta sauces piled high at the end cap down at the super market. The kid had started to skate in the redness on the floor. Oh, did she whack him."

"What did you do, when you saw it, Grampa?"

"What any good citizen would have done. I asked her if that was her kid she was spanking. I'll never forget her inglorious answer, 'You don't think I'd hit anyone else's kids this hard, would ya?'

"I guess not," I answered, and went to the checkout to get someone with a mop."

"Oh, that poor kid. She could use one of your Anger Management Workshops, ho ho."

"You mean the one my own mother forgot to attend?"

"Oh, well," Lark said, in her wisdom voice, "No one can pick their parents."

"What d'ya mean? I picked yours. And oh, the glories I have seen under your roof. I've witnessed a mother teaching a very,

very little girl how to hold a peanut and not be afraid, when feeding a squirrel, and on another day giving comfort after a tiny girl's nightmare. I saw that mother holding her kid up in the water until, with one moment's change, the kid could dog paddle away, on her own."

Lark said, "She called me her little fish, and boy, have I been swimming ever since. I better thank her for that."

He said, "You probably have already thanked her a hundred times, because I know you, and most likely ten more times, every time you get wet."

"Hey, Gramps, it's what we do. And don't you forget it was you who gave me my first bicycle lessons, running behind, holding the seat after the training wheels came off, until I could pedal away, solo and proud."

"Ah, it was nothing. You were born for water and wheels."

She said, "Do you mind if I thank you every five feet for the rest of this bike ride?"

Grampa laughed. "We have to do what we do, right?"

Lark said, "Yeah, right. I just wish more people thanked the people who have done good things for them."

"Some people are funny. I don't think it's that they're not grateful or appreciative. I think it's just that the words embarrass them. Hey, do any of those guys you counsel ever thank you?"

"Actually, they do, Grampa. They do it by referring me to other guys. I could make a bundle if I only charged $1 a session. It's my 'thang.'"

He said, "Maybe we could raise it to $2 when you're ready to buy your first convertible."

"Oh," she said, "I thought I was going to inherit your 1991 Toyota when I graduate."

"You kidding? I plan on driving it at least another ten years before the tires wear out." He got back on subject. "Well, there are a couple other mothers I know who have done good work. I'm thinking of your Grammie, for one. I've sat in the room with her putting band-aids on a kid who fell off his bike going down hill, and who was all pavement-rashed, and she was doing it without moralizing. That same mother reading to that son in a rocking chair, just a few years this side of the real rocking he would do later on a motorcycle during one of the Adirondack summers. She could comfort a daughter who got dumped by an early boy friend, and help that same daughter feel less guilty when she had to dump some other boy."

Lark said, "I'm not sure I could be the kind of mother she was. Mothers are called upon to do so many things."

Grampa stopped his bike. Lark almost rammed into him. "Stuff and nonsense, woman. You've had some of the sweetest models in the world. And a woman learns to be a good mom by seeing good moms. It's scientific."

Lark smiled and said, "Well, I like scientific. Still it sounds hard to: Stage a birthday, bake a cake, getting them to eat more than beige foods, nagging about tooth brushing, remembering to be on time when picking someone up after school. Whew. Maybe I'll stay a bachelorette."

"Well," Grampa said, pedaling fast down the path, "I doubt it. Unless there's a national pact for all boys to sign a pledge to remain bachelors. And that ain't gonna' happen.

"Hey, and don't forget, you'll always have help. And at least I'll be around for the real dirty work, like: preaching at them, clarifying, encouraging, supporting, setting limits, demanding adherence to the family values, and pushing them off to find their own troubles."

They started to ride again. Lark rode alongside of him, and looked at him pumping along. "Hey, Grampa, anyone told you lately how glad I am to have you?"

He looked over at her, and smiled and said, "Not lately, maybe three minutes ago. But, from your syrupy tone, what's this going to cost me."

"Funny you should mention, costing you. Because when we get home, Mom and I have something planned for you."

"What, what. A small shopping trip to Lord and Taylor?"

"No, Grampa, no. We think it's time for you to receive, not just to keep giving, giving, and giving."

"Yeah, I bet. And then, it's off to the Mall?"

"Calm down, boy. Let the good flow in. It's your daughter-in-law and one of your granddaughters talking here. All the stuff you bought us at Dollar General the last two times isn't anywhere near running out."

Grampa grinned. "All right, all right. I'm calm. I'm a good dog, an obedient dog, lovely dog. Woof. Woof. Let's turn around and head for home, good old home. Where the mothers don't yell, and the fathers change diapers, and you so warmly welcome me when I come to visit."

Cheap Grampa and The Thing Called Christmas

Right after Halloween, Grampa got out an email to all four kids and the six grand kids, including the one born Oct. 3rd who couldn't read yet. It was a simple statement, one he clearly believed in, truly valued. It went like this.

"Dear Offspring,

I'm asking you not to sweat over plans to come down to Florida over Christmas holiday. I don't want any of you to break your budgets, and I sure am not going to contribute elaborate air fares to something as pointless as flying down here for the holidays. You can get frisked somewhere else.

I want you to spend time close to your kids' friends, they are at those ages, and with the up-north in-laws and grandparents. It seems so logical to me. And later in the season we can work out some visits to this Floridian Grampa. Doesn't it make sense?

I love you all, thriftily.
Grampa."

The phones rang shortly after that, one after another. All with a quiet, "Thanks, Pops. It does make sense to us. The kids agree. We'll call on Christmas day, if we can get a line through to Florida. Thanks for reading our minds. We love you. And we sure remember what you did for Christmases when we were kids."

Grampa threw his head back and laughed. "You mean that idea of not letting you dive under the tree to grab your loot and rip the paper off before breakfast?"

His oldest son, Jerry, said, "Yep. That one. And my little brother got to go under the tree first, but not to get 'his' loot, but to pull out the presents he had for each of us, his greedy little siblings, and we each had to open the one he gave us, one at a time. And none of us could open ours until the little twerp told us we were next in line.

"Man, it took an hour, but it really was fun. We're doing that same thing in our family now, Pops. Thanks."

When his daughter called she sounded relieved, too. "Thanks, Dad. We were wondering how we could juggle my husband's family, who expected us, and hoped we wouldn't be flying off to Florida just to see you."

Grampa said, "I'm so smart. Thanks for seeing the wisdom, darling."

"You, you cute man, are full of wisdom. I remember how the whole Christmas day went. After Mel gave his presents, and what an idea that was, to put the emphasis, way back then, on the giver, we'd have breakfast all together, with just a few looks over at the tree, wondering what was under there for us. And I remember you had whispered to me that after breakfast, it would be my turn to give what I had made or bought for everyone else, and to give them, one at a time."

Grampa said, "Oh, I remember your face. You dressed for the occasion, with a crown your mother had found somewhere, and a special dress with sparkles all over it. You knew what a celebration was."

"Thanks, Pops. I remember I had to go change my dress, because when I was done, and before the next round of present giving, we all bundled up and went out to the commuter railroad station, about seventeen miles up the hill."

"Come on, it was five blocks, long blocks, of course, but the snow on the trees was so beautiful."

"It was. And I loved that we sang Christmas carols to the people waiting for the train. And I remember the surprise on the faces of the people getting off the train, hearing the applause for our singing."

"Your mom sure knew how to lead the singing."

And so the phone calls went, each kid remembering something special about Christmas day when they were kids, and not complaining at all about having to wait until after dinner, when they could give their presents. Because in the afternoon, in between a giving session, we all got out the guitars and Don made that cello rock the rafters, and we sang every folk song we had ever learned.

Grampa reminded them, "Hey, guys, I didn't get to give my special presents until maybe it was 8 o'clock, and you were all so sleepy, you almost didn't notice the endless time I spent making all those home-made things."

So it was, that everyone agreed to stay where they were, with promises that they'd call on Christmas day.

"Make it late in the day, please, kids."

"Why, Gramps?" the eldest of the granddaughters asked. "You got a big date or something?"

"Well, actually, I do. I volunteered to work at the Shelter. I'm on the kitchen staff for the big Christmas dinner we're going to make for about seventy-five people."

"Oh, Grampa," she said. "That's so sweet."

"Well, thanks. I'll think of you. I'm in charge of making chicken livers and onions, which probably no one at the shelter has ever eaten. I get to keep the leftovers. It comes with the territory."

"Hey," she said, "hold the onions and I'll be right down to help."

"Not this year, sweetheart. Go have a wonderful day up there, and I'll love hearing your voice on the phone after I get back. Collect some high points to tell me about. I love you all. And think of all the money we didn't have to spend for snacks at the airport."

Dog

Cheap Grandpa had really missed that college granddaughter. Robin's life as a college student and a Nanny had been totally consuming her waking days. Grampa's life, getting ready to head for Florida, didn't leave much casual time, either.

Grampa shook his head. Life just ain't simple. So often, choices ain't no ride on no pink duck. That's an allusion to a merry-go-round, where the littlest kids ride in the pink swan section, safe, predictable; and where the excitement is all in the lions and tigers and wild horses, that go up and down and from which you can grab the golden rings. You can't from the pink swan.

But, Gramps did want to see them all up in Ithaca, at least once more before he headed for the beach and Floridian decadence. So, he put his bike on the bike rack, packed his helmet, and that's how Cheap Grampa and Robin got to be on the street biking on a Friday morning, heading towards one of their favorite Dollar Stores.

Robin told him how much she, too, had missed their bike rides. She thrived on telling all the dogs and their owners how precious it was to see them as she rode by. Her words were music, as she said, "good dog, lovely dog, beautiful dog" as they passed all the dogs on their leashes. She complimented the people with the big dogs, telling them how obedient they were, which translated into that they did not drag their masters into the poison ivy.

And then it came. Robin said, "Grampa, I think you need to get a dog."

"So, why would I need to get a dog. I got a pet."

"What pet? Your orchid? I know you take care of it like it was a pet."

"I know my orchid isn't like a real pet to you. But, I told you, I already got a pet."

"Yeah, where?"

"I got all you grand kids. That's more than enough," he groaned.

"Yeah, well, that's nice, but I think you should get a dog. And then you wouldn't be lonely when I can't come down because of all the boys and other friends I need to spend my time with."

Grampa took on a look full of wistful memories. "I've had dogs. I don't want one now."

"One would be wonderful company, Grampa."

Grampa's eyes looked far away. "I had one when I was a little kid. She was such good company."

"I've never heard that story, Gramps."

"It's too sad. I don't talk about her."

"Tell me, Gramps. You know I'll listen"

"I named her Princess. She was just a mutt. Showed up in the backyard one day. I stole a hot dog from the fridge when my mom wasn't looking and gave it to her. And the dog adopted me. I begged and begged and finally, my father got on my side, and said to my mother, 'Let him have her. It'll be good for the boy.'

"I remember my mother saying, 'Well, if that dog makes any mess in this house, I'll poison it. And don't expect me to feed it. You'll collect scraps from what any boarder leaves on his plate, and the dog eats outside, not in the house, and she sleeps in the basement, and that's that.'"

"Your Mother was clear, wasn't she?"

"That's one way to put it. Well, I obeyed, and Princess didn't seem to mind. I couldn't wait to get home from school and take her off her rope and the two of us headed out for the woods, where I pretended we were Indians sent out to hunt. Princess would smell out the game and I taught myself to walk so softly, never breaking a twig to scare any deer away, and then I'd pretend my arrows would bring it down, and I would pretend to bring it back to the village and everyone would say I was a hero. We'd play that every day. Until..."

"Until what, Grampa?"

"Until the day I came home after school, and the rope was cut and Princess was gone. I called out her name all over the streets, all through the woods. I missed dinner, and went to bed hungry. And got up before everyone else was up and called her name everywhere I thought she might be."

"Oh, Gramps, that must have been so hard. You really loved Princess, didn't you?"

"Yep, I did. And I prayed every night for a month, asking God to bring her back to me, and every day after school I kept on looking for her. All the kids on our street helped me, hoping we would find her, but she never came back."

"I'm so sorry Grampa. But surely another dog came along, didn't it?"

"No, Robin honey, my mother was glad to have Princess gone. Her words were, 'I have enough mouths to feed around here.' So maybe that's why I'm not too interested when you say maybe I should have a dog. I had one, and it hurt too much when I lost her."

Robin was clearly touched, and gave Grampa a big hug. "Thanks, honey, I know you worry about me. Maybe when you come down to Florida this winter, we can find a nice alligator for a pet for Grampa."

Robin said, "I hear they only eat once a week. And I could make sure you were out of town on the day your pet alligator was up for eating."

"Or maybe we could find me a smaller lizard that would be friendly, and not eat too much. Let's just not call it Princess."

They arrived at the Dollar Store. Robin said, "One consolation, Grampa. This will be a cheap run. I won't nag you to buy me any dog food, but your story makes me miss our cat, Mookie. Maybe you could help me coax my Mom and Dad into getting us a new pet."

Grampa said, "Let's start small. We'll ask for a horse."

ALBUM NINE

EXTRAVAGANT CLAIMS

Laundry

Cheap Grampa took yesterday's socks, joined together by the ever-loyal sock disk, and banked them off the wall, right into the hamper. His granddaughter watched.

"Two points Grampa," she said.

"No way," he said, "four points. I get two extra points for every sock that is sock disked to a compatible partner. My darling granddaughter, do you know, if every human being used a sock disk on every pair of socks they throw in the laundry, there would be no one wandering around with a single sock, searching and searching for the other one."

Standing, with his hand over his heart, he proclaimed, "Let it be known, no washing machine ever eats up a pair of sock disked socks. And both of us know that on the average, in a typical household, six single socks a week are sucked down the drain of washing machines or slithered through the pipes of an average American clothes dryer. Each and every week."

She responded in her usual enthusiastic way. "Oh, Grampa that's awesome news. And just think of all the uninformed people who walk around with one blue sock and one green one because they've lost the other mate to their blue socks and green socks."

"You are right. Absolutely right, and I'm out to save America, my awesome Phoebe. Now, brace yourself, here's another way I save money. I don't wash my shirts. I just put them on this chair over here, and the next night when I get undressed, I put that shirt on top of the other shirt, and at the end of the month, I just turn the pack over and wear them back down through. Then, and only then, do I put the entire load into the washing machine."

Her mouth opened and she rolled her eyes, and just mumbled, "Grampa."

He said, "No arguments, please, because furthermore, to save money, I don't bother to use any detergent. Cold water only and cold rinse only."

She gasped and said, "But, Grampa, what about the smells, the body odor?"

"You read too many advertisements. After the age of eighty, no one smells bad. Anyhow, I hang the shirts out in the sun to dry and the sun refreshes them so it seems like a brand new morning every time I put on one of those shirts."

She went over to him, and gave him a hug. "Well, I'm glad at least you do wash your socks in a timely fashion, and I sure as heck hope you use some soap in that department."

"What? You think just because you saw this old basketball player throw some socks into a hamper that I launder them? The good socks I just put on the other chair, and at the end of the month, I turn that pile over and wear it back down through again, just like the shirts."

"Oh, Grampa, I don't believe you. I know when my mother comes and finds this out, she'll be horrified."

He said, "Don't you go squealing on me, poop deck."

She answered, "You know I'm honorable. But I know when she walks into this room, and gets a whiff of those two chairs, after she bops you on the head with a badminton racquet, she'll stand over you while you do your laundry, and with soap. She wouldn't tolerate such unhealthy habits."

"Well, she's going to have to arm wrestle with me. And only if she wins, will I let her do my socks. But, never, never, my shirts. By not washing my shirts until they've been worn twice,

I save a lot of money. That's money that will go to you some day. It's part of being frugal."

She winked at him. "You mean fragrantly frugal, and that's part of being cheap, don't you, Grampa."

Grampa said, "Frugal, schmugal, I just know I love you, and I'm doing everything I can to live as long as I can so I can be around you to enjoy you forever."

"Ok, Gramps, you get my vote. So what if you do smell a little."

"Come on, you don't believe that stuff about my not doing my laundry. I'm the poster boy for laundry for old folks. In my speeches at the nursing homes, I tell them, 'I figure, if you don't wear clothes you don't have to wash them.' I don't know why I don't get invited back again."

Hallowe'en

It was that time of the year again. The Vermont granddaughter came down for a visit and was all excited about Hallowe'en, the holiday she liked more than any other.

"Oh, Gramps, will you go out trick and treating with me when the night comes?"

"I don't know, honey. With things with the economy so bad, I think I have to stick close to home that night."

"Gramps, you mean you're really going to answer the door and give kids candy this year?"

"Well, not exactly," he answered. "Candy I don't believe in, except for you and the other grand kids. But not just for somebody I don't know who rings my doorbell with a pillow case opened wide expecting great loot."

"But my darling Grampa, that's what Hallowe'en is all about. Kids of all ages expect that."

"Expect, schmabect, I don't believe in it."

"You did believe in it once when you came to Vermont and we went out together on Hallowe'en night. I remember, but do you remember my costume that night when I was a nebula for Halloween?"

"Awesome, awesome, a word I hardly every use. You, you were it. You lit up the sky, you and your nebula. More than the sky, you were awesome to every galaxy. How I remember so enjoying walking around with you and watching everyone being dazzled."

"And you ate most of the chocolate candy before I got it home that night."

"Hey, but remember how, generously, I left you all the junk stuff, including the fruits which I believe in. Anyhow, I'm not giving out my precious candy to little kids who don't know me and I don't know. But I do want to hear about what are you going to be this year? Not much can match your nebula gig."

"I was thinking of going as a bird rehabilitation expert. I'd wear a white coat and use that stethoscope you gave me, and carry a cage, one you gave me, and inside would be a little pigeon we got with a broken leg and which the vet bandaged up in all kinds of gauze and printed band-aids."

"That's all very nice. Maybe you can get a nice turkey vulture to walk around with you that night."

"But, Gramps. You're my favorite turkey vulture. I want you."

"Honey, I'd like to, but I'm a little tired. I spent this week building this barbed wire fence all around the house."

"To keep kids from coming to your door?"

"Well, to discourage them, mostly. I don't want my outhouse knocked over if I don't give them treats."

"You're kidding. You haven't had an outhouse for years."

"I just never showed you where it was."

"Listen, Mistah, if you had one I would have found it. I know every inch of that land you call home."

"Ok, you nailed me. Caught me in another lie. I'll have to be a good boy. And maybe I'll ask you to stay with me that night instead of going out tricking and treating yourself?"

"I'm flattered, Gramps, but you know how important it is for me to be out there raking in the loot."

"I'll give you loot. You can raid my Gummy Bears and all my licorice."

She thought about that for a while, and said. "Gramps. I'll make a deal with you. I'll stay with you for the hour when the little, little kids come out for trick and treating. I'll work with you. I'll give you that one precious hour of my evening. I'll help the cute kids through the barbed wire, and make them say their name and tell you what grade in school they are. And if I know they're seventh graders, we won't give them anything. I might even direct them to go out by the creek and they can knock over your outhouse in revenge."

Gramps laughed his Cheap Grampa laugh. "And it won't cost me a cent."

"Of course, it will cost you a few cents. You have to have candy for the little ones."

"No I won't. I found this apple tree at a house where no one was home, and the back yard was loaded with apple drops. I got a bushel of them still on the back of my bike."

"Gramps, apples are out. I'm sorry."

"What, you are against nutrition and healthy living? Free apples are both of those things."

Oh, dear Gramps, you don't understand. No parent will let a kid accept an apple for trick and treat. Didn't you ever hear about the sick people who put razors in apples?"

He was shocked. "I'd never do that. I put the razors in oranges."

She gave him the dirty look. The well-rehearsed dirty look he got at least four or five times a day when she heard him say bad jokes like that.

"Ok, ok, I was just kidding. So, there can't be apples or oranges. But the fruit theme does speak about healthy things, over and above teeth rotting, and obesity enhancing candy, right?"

Grudgingly, she said, "Right."

"Now, I don't know if you know that when I was a boy, way back in Pittsburgh, we didn't say, 'Trick or Treat' in those olden days. We rang the door bells, and just said, 'Nuts, nuts, please.' And at a lot of houses, that's what they gave us. Nuts. Healthy alternatives we're looking at here. So, all week, in between building the barbed wire fence, I've been rounding up some nuts for Halloween night."

"I get the joke. You mean some human nuts like me and my cousins? Is that it?"

"No, silly goose, I've been rounding up real nuts. I got a great bag of acorns we can give kids, and teach them how Native Americans ate a lot of them on Halloween night." His grin was as wide as a wide-open pillow case.

"Oh, Grampa, that's cheap all right. But you can't give today's American children squirrel food. No, no, acorns won't do the 'nut' thing for Halloween night."

Quickly, he goes to his plan B. "On my way home the other day, I went by this big tree, and underneath, lovely nuts in a kind of spiny shell. Someone told me they were chestnuts. How would that do for the treats part of 'trick or treat'?"

"Gramps, you and I both know those are horse chestnuts. They're really buckeyes, and as far as I know, they're not quite edible. And both of us will get all cut up on the spines, just trying to get the nuts out."

"Well, there go all my good intentions. No apples, no acorns, and now no chestnuts. So much for healthy alternatives."

"And that means that you'll give kids candy when they come to your door."

"No, it just means that I'm going to go out with you and you can put a leash on me, and make a sign for my back that says, *Turkey Vulture. Do not feed.*"

"Oh, Gramps, that's my wildest dream, but knowing you, there will be some 'condition' I'll have to meet before I get my wildest dream. Tell me."

"Well, I was just thinking. Maybe, half way through our night, we can take the stuff you got and go back to my house, real quick, and I'll have a basket by my front door, and we put half of your treasures into that basket."

"Half of my candy, Gramps? Oh no."

"And the nuts, too. Conditions are conditions. And you'll have to help me make a sign that says: THIS IS THE HONOR SYSTEM. *You can take something out, but you have to put something in. So if you take three pieces of candy out of here, you have to put three pieces from your previous loot collection into my basket.* And we have to make one more sentence on the sign: *Because tomorrow we're going to take this basket to an Orphanage where the kids weren't able to do trick and treat.* Does that sound fair?"

"Gramps, it sounds fair and it sounds cheap, just like you. No wonder I love you sooo much. I agree. But, should we add to the sign: *Please, no apples or oranges. And if you don't like this idea, you can go knock my outhouse over. It's down by the creek.*"

"Agreed. Now, get the magic marker. And where's my leash?

Grampa and Phoebe Go To a Restaurant

"Grampa, you are really going to take me to a restaurant?"

"Yes, so what's so unusual?" he smiled.

"It's never happened before, for one thing, and for another the other grand kids have been talking, and none of them has ever gone to a restaurant with you."

"That's no surprise. Of course, why would I spend money at a restaurant when I can cook it at home, cheaper, and with more sanitariness."

"Is that a word?"

"Of course it's a word. I made it up."

"Oh, Grampa. I'm so honored. Am I dressed right? Do I have to get fancy?" Not really vain. She works too hard with all those birds and wounded mammals to be vain. But still she says. "How do I look Gramps?"

"Like your mother, and that's good. Did she see you in those shoes? I see they have eight inch high heels."

She got a little shy for a moment. "Well, not exactly."

"Not exactly? It is or it isn't. What's the issue here?"

"Oh, Gramps, she thinks I'm not ready for high heels. But this 'going to a restaurant' thing with you, it's no small thing, so I really wanted to do it up big."

"It wouldn't be big with nice flip flops?"

"Oh, Grampa, you don't understand. I'm still a kid, but I am growing up."

"But in those shoes your toes stick out. I can't take you to a restaurant and your feet look all naked." That's when she gave him that special look again, the one that could freeze pigeons in flight. "All right. You're beautiful. People will quit eating and wonder who the movie star is with her toes sticking out." He paused a minute and said, "You look just right, now let's get to the joint. Am I driving or are you driving?"

"I'm thirteen years old, and I don't drive, Grampa, you know that."

"Ok, we'll take our bikes. It's right along the bike path, this restaurant joint I want to take you to."

"I got all dressed up to ride my bike?" Her hands went to her hips. A statement was made.

"You can ride side saddle. It will work out." She gave him another one of The Looks. And a really fierce one.

"Just kidding. We need the car."

"How come? Are we going far?"

"Nah."

"Well, where are we going?"

"Just to the drive-in at McDonald's. They don't let you walk through." And then he gave *her* the look, smiled and said, "Just kidding."

Hands still on the hips, she said, "You better be kidding."

Her mother, my favorite and only daughter, came in the room just before they were to leave for the restaurant. She looked Phoebe over, smiled, and said, very softly, "Not those shoes."

Phoebe moved right into her little lawyer mode. "Oh, Mom. They match my outfit. Grampa said we're going to a special joint." She looked at Grampa to get his usual support.

He smiled and simply said, "Change your shoes, or I'll make you go by bicycle."

Without protesting further, or submitting yet one more brief, she laughed and said, "Court is adjourned, I'll be right down in my sensible sandals."

Her mom said, "Thanks, honey. I picked a flower for your hair." Phoebe put it right behind her ear and went up to get her sandals. It made her look extra beautiful.

"You're a good mom, kid."

"Thanks, and I appreciate your help. You always read it right. So, where are you taking her?"

"To McDonald's." And he laughed. "No, we're going to a genuine Chinese Buffet, of the 'All you can eat' variety."

"And I know why, you cheap fox," she said. "Because you don't have to be waited on and you don't have to leave a tip."

"Hey, you know me better than that. I'm cheap, but never to a waitress. She'll get twenty percent like I hope everyone else gives to her."

"But, how come? All she does is bring you a pot of tea."

"But she brings cups and water, too, and big smiles, and she doesn't mind how many plates I use or how many times I go for seconds, thirds and fourths. Anyhow, she's a young mother. I saw two of her kids coloring and reading in one of the booths when I was there the last time."

"What, you've been there before? I thought you never go to

restaurants because you can cook it at home better, cheaper and..."

"Even more sanitary," he finished her sentence. "I went once for practice. I'm going to take all the grand kids, eventually, one at a time, in the near future."

"Well, big spender, flashy dresser. Next it will be Las Vegas."

"Over my dead body," he said, just as Phoebe came back.

"Don't anybody die on my behalf, please."

"I promise," Grampa said, "And don't you really look like a princess, like someone who makes reservations rather than cooks."

"Bad joke, Gramps. Besides, I cook plenty. Right, mom?"

"Yeah, right. And we all appreciate it."

Phoebe said, "Thanks," and turning to her Grampa, asked a question. "Does this joint you're taking me to, this place called a restaurant, where you never take anyone, need for us to make a reservation?"

"No, it's so bad, there's never a crowd, except sometimes a couple of people picketing the place, complaining about the slave labor in the kitchen. Your sandals seem just right," he added.

"Oh, fine. Will we have to join the picketers?"

"No, not until we eat."

Mom said, "He told me where you're going and I think it's perfect."

Grampa said, "Perfect, yeah. They don't have a menu, which is one of the reasons I like the place."

"No menu?" Phoebe looked puzzled. "How do we know what to order?"

"You'll see. And I love that there is no menu so I don't have to spend all that time reading only the right hand column to see what's the cheapest thing to eat."

"No menu, no prices? What is it, you cook your own food, and just pay them for stove time?"

Mom asked, "You mind if I tell her, Pops? I'd like her to be relaxed when she walks in."

"I'll tell her." He took Phoebe's hands in his, looking overly cheerful as he said, "Honey, it's out in the woods. We eat in the kitchen of a slaughterhouse, where you get to eat the deer some hunter has just shot. Sometimes, it still has the fur on it when they serve it to you. The restaurant's called, 'Bambies.'"

"Dad, stop that. You're impossible. Phoebe, it's a marvelous Chinese Buffet. You remember, we went to one once? Everything's laid out in rows, food in hot pans, and then salads and watermelon and other fruits, on cold trays laid out in another set of rows. And they have tags to tell you what's in each pan."

Gramps grinned, "Only in this place the tags are all in Yiddish because the place is run by a nice Jewish couple, the Horowitz's."

Phoebe said, "Very funny, Grampa. I can't wait to see the Horowitz's Chinese Buffet faces."

Mom said, "He's such a joker, and you're growing up just like him. Well, anyhow, you can pick from all the stuff, and get just what you want."

Phoebe said, "A perfect place to break my visual eating habit, huh, Gramps?"

"Hmm. You see right through me. No, I have such faith in you. This evening is without moralizing, just for fun."

"But, Gramps, I like it when you teach me something."

He gave her a hug and said, "Thanks for the validation, but tonight I need you to teach me how to use chopsticks."

"Sure, and I bet by fortune cookie time, you'll be awesome."

Mom said, "I think you two better get going before all the shrimp are gone."

Gramps interrupted, "There'll be plenty of everything. They never seem to run out. It could be that the food is so bad, but anyhow, Phoebe, it's an 'eat all you can stuff in your mouth' kind of place. In that gracious ambience, you can just go back as many times as you want, and best of all, you get all that for one set price. You see why it's my kind of place. Not only that, they give you a clean plate each time, if you like. We'll be there until midnight just so we can get our money's worth."

"Money's worth. Those are two magical words to me. Grampa, stop crying. You know I'm cheap like you. I can't wait, Gramps. Mom, which drawer did you put my chop sticks in?"

Cheap Grampa knew it was going to be a wonderful night. He was already figuring out a way to bring back doggie bags for each of them. "Hey, I got it. Phoebe could go play with the little kids in the back booth, distracting the mother who would go see what was making them all laugh, and I could then stuff things into the plastic bags I brought in my overcoat's pockets. Bet no one had ever thought of that at a Chinese Buffet."

Cheap Grampa at the Post Office

The Post Office closes at 4:30 p.m. Cheap Grampa has the reputation of getting there at 4:29 p.m. with almost a religious reliability. "We can close, girls, CG is here. Time to go home."

He always says, "I can close the gate for you, if you need help. I just have a few things to mail."

But when he entered today, there was no one on line, and actually, no other car was out at the parking lot. Cheap Grampa almost thought his watch might have been slow, or worse, today was a holiday he had missed.

"Slow day, Ms. Postmistress," he asked?

"No, not really, but you can finish the day by brightening it up, as always. What you got, Gramps?"

"Thanks," and he bowed. "This is just a box of presents for the new grandson, born midnight, Sunday."

"Well, well," she said. "Congratulations. So what are you sending him?"

"A couple of stuffed animals."

"Looks like more than a dozen teddy bears in a box this size."

Grampa grinned. "Well, you know me. There's also a book in there for my daughter-in-law on how to handle the first day of school."

"That will give her six years to get it read. Smart giving, Grampa. And for the son?"

Cheap Grampa thumped the box. "Oh, a couple of books for him, one is on coaching little league baseball. Another on

'Making Your Child a Safe Driver.'"

"Very timely," she said. "We could use a few more safe teenage drivers."

"I haven't forgotten he's still a baby. So I built him a mobile to hang over the crib. It's made from beer cans I painted, and in a strong wind they make lovely sounds."

She laughed, "I didn't know you were a beer drinker."

"I'm not, I fished them out of the stuff at the dump. When I was out there, I also found a slightly rusted tricycle. I've already cleaned it up and repainted it fire engine red. But, it's not in the box."

"That's good," she said, "because this box is going to cost you $24.68, Priority. Shame the kid lives all the way in Florida. And, knowing you, since the kid is in no rush, we can ship it parcel post for $12.98. Do we got a deal?"

"That's poifect, madame. And there is nothing liquid, fragile, terroristic or anything flammable in it. Oh, oh, there *is* a cup, but I wrapped it in layers of bubble wrap. It says, 'The Best Momma.'"

"Nice going. She's lucky to have a F.I.L. like you."

Grampa scuffed his foot and said, "Aw, shucks. I hope she likes the button I painted for her. It says, 'The Baby's Crying. Nurse him, stupid.'"

"Yeah, that will go over big, I'm sure. Oh, by the way, what did they name the boy?"

"They just call him 'Boy' right now. They got into lots of arguments about names. Just couldn't arrive at a decision. Anyhow, they're very moderne, and plan to wait a month to see if he tells them what name he wants, that is if they decide to keep him or not."

The postmistress looked shocked. "What? Until they decide if they're going to keep him or not?"

"I told you they were moderne. Just kidding. They love him so much, already. They'll raise him well, with lots of touching, cuddling, and hugs, and boundless validations. Just good love."

She made a not so sneaky look at her wristwatch. "Getting beyond closing time, Gramps. Anything else to mail? Need some cash?"

"Oh, thanks. Yes, I could use fifty dollars, two twenties and a ten, please. I'll swipe my card, and hope I remember my pin number. Oh, I just remembered two other things that are in the box. There's a tape of some of the Nanny shows from TV, and two fountain pens."

She handed him the bills, and the slip to sign. "Here you go. I can understand the Nanny tapes, but what's with the fountain pens?"

"For his Bar Mitzvah, silly. He'll be thirteen in no time, and just in case I'm not around, every Grampa gives the Bar Mitzvah boy a fountain pen, on the day he becomes a man."

"Yeah, I heard about that. But one customer came in the other day and told me that his Bar Mitzvah boy handed it back to his Grampa and said, 'Gramps, I really need an iPad, instead.'"

Grampa shook his head in dismay. "Not my kid. If I'm around he'll be glad to get a fountain pen, because I know he'll be a writer, like his dad is."

"That's sweet," she said. "But how come two fountain pens?"

"Well, like his dad, he'll probably lose the first one before he learns to be more careful. See you tomorrow. I hope you'll personally fly that box down to Florida, with your usual, 'We aim to please, U.S. Postal Service way.'"

"Especially for you, Cheap Grampa. See you tomorrow at 4.29 p.m."

"Maybe, I'll turn over a new leaf. I'll try for 4:28. Nighty night."

And she pulled the gate behind him. "Congratulations, again, Gramps."

ALBUM TEN

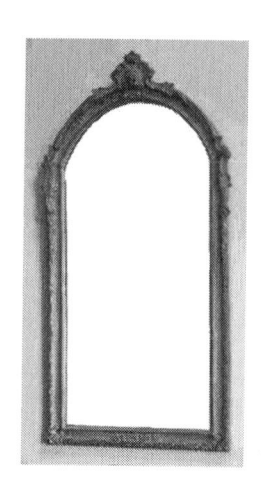

REFLECTIONS

Peaches

Cheap Grampa woke up one morning and said to himself, "I'm going to live this day with a focus on my Infinite Potential."

He curled up in bed and thought about it. Infinite was easy. That simply meant a lot of something, and then a whole lot more. Lots and lots of lots of something would surely be infinite.

Feeling a little draft, he pulled up the blanket and thought some more. "For example if I biked out to where there were all those peaches that had dropped to the ground, and no one seemed to be there looking after them, I could bring along a bushel basket and fill it with an infinite numbers of peaches.

"And when I got home I could make infinite batches of peach compote, or an infinite number of peach pies. Of course, if I got caught by the police, I might have to spend lots and lots of infinite nights in jail." Unlikely, Cheap Grampa thought. "The cops know me. They would listen to my story about how I was out there, crying out loud about how those peaches were being wasted and I was planning on bringing a peach cobbler over to the station for some of their coffee breaks."

Now, Cheap Grampa didn't want to become someone who lived with infinite lies. So, in reality, if the cops caught him he would tell the whole truth. That peach orchard had been deserted. Of course he didn't really ask very many people if they knew where the owners went to and why they hadn't harvested their peaches. The land was almost covered with drops. No one else was ever there when I was picking. It seems there aren't infinite numbers of people interested in dropped peaches. At least at midnight. So, I must seize the potential and bring home as many as I can. After all, infinite isn't that complex.

But that now took Cheap Grampa to the whole concept of

potential. As he lay there in bed, thoughts kept running through his mind. A big idea grew before him. "Just what is the potential behind this Cheap Grampa gig I'm on? I really retired with enough money to not ever have to be cheap. I don't really need to keep making homemade presents for the grand kids. I don't have to keep buying things to bring home, that were things I didn't really need but that I had seen on sale, or that were being given away from the free tarps at the Flea market.

"But on the other hand there is, indeed, something with enormous potential about being the Cheap Grampa. As that sweet geezer, I sort of serve as a mirror to hold up to the grand kids and some of their friends, a mirror that keeps asking good questions. Values questions like: 'What is money for anyhow? How much money will ever be enough? Can you get trapped into thinking that money is happiness, or popularity, or even worse, that it can buy you love?'"

He didn't want to contribute to more of those buy-me-gimme-get-me kids the world seems to have in such infinite numbers. "Potential has to be filled with stuff more important than money. Potential requires that values inform our choices, that they are laced with morality, and slathered with a boundless amount of compassion and hope, and serious actions about social justice."

That thought felt so satisfying that Cheap Grampa turned over, pulled up the blanket higher, and mumbled, "I'll just rest a little, but I must not forget that today is trash day, and I only have an hour to get ready before I go roaming around the garbage cans out on my route, my infinite route, the one with all that infinite potential."

Leaving Florida

Thanks to the brilliance of the Democrats in Congress who passed a Social Security program for Grampa types, the retired ones, guaranteed over sixty-five, (and that's Cheap Grampa, lucky me,) I get to live in two parts of the country every year. Well, Social Security, even after working fifty-two years as a teacher, can't do that alone. I also have some teacher retirement funds that come in every month.

Being cheap, I invested over the years and like the other guiltless rich, paid off the mortgages on both houses, and now, really, only have to deal with electricity, phone, oil, gas, garbage removal, sewer bills, and things called real estate taxes, plus a few other etc's.

When asked how I'm doing financially, I smile, and say, "I'm comfortable, thank you." Of course, I don't know for how long, so I live as cheaply as I can. When you visit me in the summer, don't count on air conditioning. I hand you a cardboard fan and tell you to wave it. My granddaughter came to visit, and she dislocated her shoulder waving her fan.

Just before I went to Florida, she came to my place up north for a special Going South visit, and the weather had turned frosty. I wouldn't turn on any heat, and she almost got frostbite on her nose, inside the house. I told her she should have worn an extra pair of earmuffs to cover her nose. Or, "Go find your summer fan. Breaking down the cold air keeps it from doing frostbite. Still air is what bites. So, wave, baby, wave."

So, you see, I'm kind of intractable. And cheap, but I live pretty darn good. The winter months are spent in Florida. I have a fine bike down there, and almost every day head to the beach that is on the Gulf of Mexico. It's a gentle beach, and dozens of families come with little kids. It's for sure, no surfer's beach. On average, a wave of two feet is almost viewed as a tropical storm wave. One day, some joker ran up the beach yelling, "Surf's up. Surf's up," and some local wag said, "Where, Hawaii?"

But, when that granddaughter came to visit, I saw what the Gulf was invented for. She, that granddaughter, is a natural dolphin, an un-beached whale, a whole school of holy mackerel. She is a natural in water. Belly whopping away, staying under water with her goggles longer than humans are supposed to and swimming even better than any of the fish around her.

One problem is that she doesn't know when to come out of the water. She promises, begging for just fifteen more minutes and then fifteen minutes more after that. And almost always, on the first day to the beach, she gets so sunburned we have to take emergency measures for the next two days. So on those days, we dress her in long sleeved shirts and pants and a big, big hat, and we don't go to the beach, we go birding. Not your usual birding, but we do that, too. For the first birding we go to the Parrot Show at the local trailer park.

There, with no hoopla, a parrot lover performs every morning at 10 a.m. She gives a lecture and lets the frequent flyer families come and hold a parrot on their shoulders, or on top of their heads. Some of the most beautiful faces I have ever seen have been little five or six year olds with a parrot sitting quietly on their arm when they hold it just right.

Well, my granddaughter is perfectly at home, and the parrots know it. She draws them like magnets. Libby, the parrot woman, sees it, too. I predict that somewhere down the line, my kid will be delivering those 10AM lectures and teaching little kids how to keep the parrots quiet on their arms.

The other birding is at the giant National Wildlife Center. Birds are everywhere there. Most people's favorites are the Roseate Spoonbills. A flush of red, as a covey of them fly by, is thrilling, and then to watch them use that spoon bill to feed in the marshlands is unforgettable.

So with the sunburn, and no parrot bites, and without spoonbills, we have to stay home and bore ourselves with mere reading, doing crafts and baking and cooking up a storm. What fun to have a kid like that around. When she leaves, and we get her to the airport, it takes everything I got to gently wave goodbye to her. She blows me a kiss, and the damn thing stays on my forehead like some giant Macaw had scarred me for life. For life. I can barely wave back. But I do, because she's forever.

AND ALSO.....

?????

Guess What

A Short Play featuring Phoebe and Cheap Grampa

P- Guess what, Grampa?
GP- You're gonna get married.
P- No, no. I may never get married.
GP- Guess what?
P- What?
GP- I just don't believe you. You are a perfect candidate for a lifetime of marital bliss.
P- Well I don't know about that. He'd have to love cats.
GP- Hell, most male types are dumb enough to love cats if their girlfriend loves cats.
P- That's not what I mean. He'd have to *really* love them.
GP- So, what's the test of that? Oh, how about putting the cat box under his side of the bed.
P- Guess what?
GP- What? You've already had a boy sleeping in your bed and you put a cat box under his side of the bed.
P- Oh you silly goose. He was a guest and I gave him my room, but because we were crowded, we had to put the cat box somewhere.
GP- How did it work out?
P- The cats were happy, and he didn't even notice. They already have cats all around his house.
GP- So we have to think of a harder test. Guess what?
P- What?
GP- He'd have to stay up all night with you on a night when one of your cats was having kittens.
P- Oh, I wouldn't ask him to do that.
GP- Well, why not? Next thing you'll be telling me that when you have a baby he wouldn't be willing to stay up all night to watch and help, and maybe faint?
P- Guess what?
G- What?
P- I'm not sure about marrying, but I'm even less sure that I

want to go through all that pain to have children.
GP- Sure, you'll make a kitten go through it, but not you. Is that fair?
P- Well, it's not the same, Grampa.
GP- Guess what?
P- What?
GP- I have it upon authority of my granddaughter who loves animals, that animals have all kinds of feelings just like humans have. Like loneliness, like, you know, home-coming eagerness, like worrying about their siblings, like, you know some of them are faithful forever and ever to their mates. Like they *feel*, my granddaughter argues.
P- Guess what?
GP- What?
P- All right, points well taken. But if you use one more "like, you know, like" I'm going to send you back to spend the rest of your days with adolescents.
GP- Ok, but my point's 'well taken'? Brilliant you should have said, since they were all your points. And I think this man should have been sent to law school. So well argued, with premise delivered and logical points made right up to collecting a fee for the gifts given.
P- Guess what?
GP- What?
P- I love you. And maybe I'll name my first child after you.
GP- Sure, and with my luck you'll have a daughter just like you.
P- Your name can be a boy's name or a girl's name.
GP- Well, I've just changed it to Algernon, the Cheap.
P- I can call her Algie, can't I?
GP- Guess what?
P- What?
G- Yes you can. And forever. Because I love you sooo much.
P- You just have to get the last word in, don't you?
G- Guess what?
P- What?
G- I do.

IN THE END

Catastrophe

Cheap Grampa called his granddaughter. His voice was shaking, there was a deep sadness that she heard in his trembling voice. Something had happened.

"Oh, Grampa, what's wrong? Did you fall off your bicycle? Were you wearing your helmet?"

Grampa said, "About helmets, it's not even a question. And, no, no, my bicycle is great. I got a new wheel. I'm not even riding on the spokes any more. I didn't fall off my bicycle. But if you don't come ride with me, soon, I just might fall off my bicycle and then you'll have to ride yours to the hospital to visit me."

"Oh, Gramps. I'm worried. What else could it be, Grampa?"

"Are you ready for this? I don't know how to tell you. I've been sick with the news all morning."

"What, Grampa, what? Did one of your old friends die this morning? I'd be so sad."

"No, no. All my old friends have already died, it's not that, honey."

"Well, tell me, what, what is it Grampa? You sound so sad. I'm worried. Should we drive right down? I'll tell my mom and dad."

"No, no, you have all those birds to take care of. I'll be all right. It helps that I could just call and tell you about it. Already, I feel better. But it sure knocked me for a loop. Oy vey."

"Yes, you talked, but you still haven't said what it is. Grampa, please tell me. I'll put us on speaker phone so mom can hear too."

"Mom, Mom," she called. "It's Grampa, and something horrible's happened to him."

"No, no," Grampa said. "It's not horrible, at least it wouldn't be to most other people. Don't get worried, daughter."

"What is it, Dad? You sound awful. Are you hurt? Did you fall? Were you wearing your helmet?"

"How come you two always worry about me and a helmet? You know how committed I am to helmets. I always wear one when I bike."

"Yeah, Grampa, but such a cheap helmet, made out of a large yogurt cup. We do worry."

"Ok. Ok, I didn't fall. It's just that.... It's only because.... I can't say it."

"Dad, Dad, Grampa, Grampa," both of them in chorus said, "Tell us. Tell us."

"Ok, Ok, let me sit down. No, I need a drink of water first. And then, I'll sit down."

"Dad, Dad, for God's sake, tell us. What is it?"

"Ok. Ok, I'll tell you. But, to a cheap guy like me, it's a catastrophe."

"What, what? Did some one break into your house and steal something? Did someone try to cheat you?"

"No, no one did any of that. I didn't lose any money at all. But, but...."

His granddaughter broke in. "Grampa, Grampa, cut the melodrama. What happened. Just tell us straight. We're grownups."

"All right. I'm ready. Are you ready? One two three." His voice cracked, and it came out small, and weak. "My life as we all have known it, is ruined. It's all down hill from here. I'm desolate."

" Please, Dad. Dad, please just tell us. We'll get in the car and come to you immediately."

"Well, you better bring the registration and the original bill of sale."

"Why, why. Are you in such desperation, we'll have to sell our car?"

"No, no, you will be able to buy a new car and a new truck, too, just like on your wish list."

"What? What do you mean?"

"I may cry when I tell you. But I have just been told I won the Publishers Clearing House Sweepstakes."

"You what?"

"I already told you." Loud sobs followed, noises of his nose being blown. "I won the Publishers' Clearing House Sweepstakes. I'm rich. I'm no longer the Cheap Grampa. It's all over." And he really started to cry, while his daughter and granddaughter jumped up and down and danced all around the telephone that was still on speaker phone, singing, "We still love you. And you still will always be our Cheap Grampa, no matter how rich you are."

Acknowledgements

First and foremost, I take my hat off to the five grand children, no longer just kids, who populate these stories. They were my muses, my inspiration, my gifts. I hope I captured their spirits, some of their words, and certainly the things they had to teach me. They are my legacy. I pray they pass on all that we shared.

They are Emma Coty, Jacob Miller, Rosie Simon, Kenzey Simon, and Sophia Parker. Right now they live scattered, from Long Island, NY, Winter Park, FL, Westchester County, NY, Ithaca, NY to Addison, VT. But they will all show up this summer in Whately, MA for the annual family reunion, with their parents' siblings, everyone's dogs, boyfriends, cats, birds, etc., to join in with the fifteen people badminton games, two shuttlecocks in the air, and everyone pitching in to shuck corn, mind the mulch, do clean ups, whatever else is needed, and the music. Wonderful music, filled with memories of all kinds.

Next, I have to say a heartfelt thanks to Marianne Preger-Simon. The sensitive and powerful editor, the true guiding star on this project and the one before it. Without Marianne, I would be just a story teller, not a published story teller.

My four kids, related as they are to the grand kids in these stories, important men and woman in highly useful roles in this world, read most of the stories, lent their wisdom and encouraged as only fully grown adults can do. There's Matt Simon, published author, entrepreneur, ex-moto cross racer, father of the newest grand kid, Andre, 6 months old and two toothed, at this time. There's Julianna up in Vermont, math teacher, wise nutrition scholar and fabulous cook, the mother of Sophia, the youngest animal and bird re-habilitation person in the state. Doug, master musician, maybe the most popular teacher in the alternative high school he works at in California. John, another master musician, teacher, disk jockey king of the 60's and 70's, stepfather of Emma and father of Jake, Rosie and Kenzey. I have a right to be proud, and full of gratitude for what they give back to me.

I must shout a resounding thanks to my writers' group up north. The weekly Sunday night sessions, writing from two different stimulators or prompts, with cookies and tea in between, usually got me two stories a night. And that's because there is no criticism, only abundant and enthusiastic encouragement and support. Think about that. Do you need to find a group like that? You'd get two keepers a night.

There are so many others who lent something to these pages: the smoker we met at the bridge; the lady with the blue hair at the yogurt cooler; my friend, the lady at the dump; the post mistress. I can't mention you all. But, please, please, feel my gratitude when you recognize yourself. And you, too, Dave Longey, who gave so much technical support so graciously to Marianne Preger-Simon, my editor and producer. Thanks again to Emil Neuman for the cover photograph. He could not have done it without the help of his wife Judy.

I'll look for you all when we bring out the sequel to <u>Cheap Grampa in Action</u>. Maybe it will be about when Cheap Grampa Gets Rich. Or when he just Goes to a Real Restaurant or Moves to Haight Ashbury.

About the Author

Sidney B. Simon is internationally known for his pioneering work in Values Clarification, and he retired as Professor Emeritus from the University of Massachusetts in 1998. Over one hundred articles and some thirteen books authored or co-authored came out of that adventurous academic life.

He was a much-in-demand keynote speaker at major conferences on Psychology, Counseling, Education, Alcohol and Drug Addiction, Self Esteem and Family Values all over the United States, Canada and in six countries in Europe.

Simon was a guest expert on the Oprah Show, and also shared his wisdom on a Phil Donahue program about fathers and sons, in the same year that he was a keynoter at the Betty Ford Clinic.

More recently, Dr. Simon has been active in the Florida literary arts community. Simon is a frequently published poet, a drama critic for the Sanibel Captiva Islander, a participant for the past five years in ART POEMS, and in 2011 he won the Lee County Literary Artist of the Year Award.

Deep down, he just wants to be nominated for the Grampa of the Year Award.

Made in the USA
Charleston, SC
16 May 2012